Walking
North 1

GW01459535

Seventeen Walks

From Hexham

To the source

J.B.Jonas

Foreword:

Those of you who have enjoyed the Tyne and South Tyne with JB's "Walking the Tyne", as well as those who haven't yet sampled our lovely Northern rivers, now have a chance to find out more about its other half - the North Tyne. Its valley is very different to the South Tyne's with echoes of its Reiver past, beautiful Kielder Water and vast Wark Forest, to name but some of its attractions. I consider myself lucky to live in this part of the world and now feel the urge to get out and explore my local river more strongly than ever. I am never disappointed and am constantly surprised by it. With JB's helpful guide, I hope you will be too."

Carol Malia
BBC Look North

The North Tyne on Walk 17

July 2005

Maps and Photographs: Nick Lord
Printed by: NW Printers

ISBN 1 901184 82 X

Contents

Acknowledgements

We would not be able to walk the paths in this book were it not for the efforts of the organizations who maintain, signpost and waymark them. I am particularly indebted to Tim Fish and Kevin Storey of Northumberland County Council, Jonathan Farries of the Forestry Commission and Lorna Lazzari and Kim Hobson of Northumberland National Park, for general advice and support also to Paul Nichols of Kielder Forest Enterprise and John Sadler of Bellingham Heritage Centre. I would also like to thank Carol Malia very much for the foreword.

I am extremely grateful to Nick Lord of Mowden Hall School who has translated my handwritten maps into the printed versions you see in the book and has done all the typing and layout. Without his skill and enthusiasm this book would not have been possible.

I would also like to thank my wife Mary and others of our family – Mick, Sara and James – for walking many of the walks with me and for their patience as I took notes and explored alternative routes.

All the maps are based on Ordnance Survey 1:25000 Outdoor Leisure Maps 42 (Kielder Water) and 43 (Hadrian's Wall) and are reproduced from Ordnance Survey mapping on behalf of the Controller of Her Majesty's Stationery Office © Crown Copyright MC 0100030976.

The Northumberland National Park Authority, The Kielder Forest Enterprise and the Rambler's Association have all contributed towards the funding of this book. I am extremely grateful for their generous support.

Preface

Those of you who have read my book "Walking the Tyne" may remember the reasons I gave for making its subject the South rather than the North Tyne. However, I did add "the North Tyne Valley is beautiful and should be explored". I have, over the past year or so, followed that piece of advice and this book is the result. The North Tyne is very different to the South Tyne, so walking it is a different, but equally rewarding experience, with all sorts of unexpected bits of landscape, a good deal of it, as with the South Tyne, linked to a former railway line. It is very much a Northumbrian valley with its echoes of the border skirmishes in its castles and bastles and if you talk to local people you still get that sense of a tough, close-nit, yet friendly, community with a pride in North Tynedale that is still very evident.

As with my other book the aim is to shadow the river (or the shores of Kielder Water through which the North Tyne flows) wherever a Right of Way exists, but also to provide walks which make the most of the best of the countryside through which the river runs.

The North Tyne starts (or rather finishes!) at Watersmeet some 2 miles west of Hexham. If you want to see where it merges with its Southern colleague into the main Tyne then, during Walk 1, turn left down Acomb's Main Street and across the A6079 into Howford Lane. Where, after about half a mile, the lane turns right, continue straight ahead under the old railway bridge to the river bank and there you are. A path does continue a short way upstream to Warden Rapids, but it is not a Right of Way so you do have to retrace your steps to Acomb. We next join the river on Walk 3.

Apart from, I hope, providing some very attractive walks this book also seeks to encourage you to explore more widely in the Northumberland National Park, Kielder Forest and Kielder Water, which have opened up North Tynedale not just to walkers. There is a wide and increasing range of activities for people of all ages and abilities, about which you can read on page 43 as the walks take you to them.

I have included rather more local history than I did in 'Walking the Tyne'; accurately, I hope. This is, of course, a walk book first and foremost, but I felt a little more in the way of a guide to this lovely, but all too little known, area would be appreciated.

How to use the book

Individual walks

14 of the 17 walks are circular, i.e. a "round" starting and finishing in the same places. Walks 4 and 15 are linear ("one way") walks linking main walks. Walk 16 is linear along the shore of Kielder Water.

Each walk is accompanied by a detailed map and full description of the route, but it is a good idea to take Ordnance Survey maps as well, for a wider picture of the countryside around you.

The "vital statistics" (distance, time, terrain, car parking, refreshments) are given for each walk and more general information about public transport and accommodation later in this introduction. I have given rather more detail about opening times in the remote areas.

The long distance walker from Hexham to Deadwater should follow the outward leg of each walk (except for walk 7 where it is the final leg) and clear instructions are given as to when you can continue from one walk to the next. The linear mileage shown on the maps and the broader route arrowheads give further guidance.

Experienced walkers know their own capabilities, so I have not suggested any stages or timings. However, if you are coming from a distance and wanted to do the whole 47½ miles in two or three days, it may be helpful to know that there are Youth Hostels at Acomb (Walk 1), whence you could visit Waters-meet as your starting point, Bellingham (Walk 10) and the Riever's Rest bunk-house at Kielder.

Accommodation

Details from Tourist Offices at Hexham and Bellingham.

Public Transport

Hexham is well served by bus and train from Newcastle and Carlisle.

Buses: To/from Newcastle: Arriva Service 602 (½ hourly), Arriva/Stagecoach 685 (hourly), Tyne Blue Line (TBL) 74 – a longer, scenic route – 2 hourly. To/from Carlisle: Service 685.

Trains: Newcastle to Hexham ½ hourly, from Carlisle hourly.

Buses to the starting points of the walks: TBL 74 operates from Hexham and Newcastle. Hadrian's Wall Bus A122 has one early morning departure from Newcastle and a late evening return, and for the rest of the day runs to/from Hexham. All the other buses (except 714 – see below) run to/from Hexham.

Walks 1,2 and 3 (Acomb and Wall): service AD122, TBL74, TBL and Tyne Valley Coaches (TVC) 880 approximately hourly.

Walks 4,5 and 6 (Chollerford, Barrasford and Gunnerton): TBL74

Walks 7 and 8 (Wark): TBL and TVC880 approximately hourly.

Walk 9 has no convenient public transport.

Walks 10 and 11 (Bellingham): TBL and TVC880 approximately hourly.

Buses don't operate late into the evening except on Fridays and Saturdays. Sunday services are sparse.

Walks 12 to 17: Public transport is infrequent beyond Bellingham though care-ful planning should enable you to find suitable connections with most of the walks. A useful bus is Arriva 714 ("The Kielder Bus") operating late May to October on Sundays from Newcastle to Bellingham and Kielder and back, and shuttling along Kielder Water in between. For other buses phone Traveline 0870 6082608 or visit a local Tourist Office.

Maps

Most maps are to scale (1:25000) but an occasional liberty has been taken with the scale where page size is a constraint.

The Calvert Trust

Kielder Water and Forest have a wealth of activities which, thanks to the Calvert Trust, are now available too to people with disabilities. What is the Calvert Trust?

Raisley Calvert, who died of TB in 1796 aged only 21, was a childhood friend of William Wordsworth, and his early encouragement was a major factor in the development of Wordsworth's poetry. The Calvert family also provided a house for the poet. By 1974 this house was owned by John Fryer-Spedding of Mirehouse on the shores of Bassenthwaite Lake. Thinking back, perhaps, to Raisley Calvert's illness, Mr. Spedding decided to turn the Calvert's house into a centre staffed and equipped to help people with disabilities to enjoy his beloved Lake District. It has been a great success ever since, and when Kielder Water was created, it seemed an ideal setting for another Calvert Centre. It was opened in 1984 and now has ten luxury chalets as well as its original cabin accommodation. Designed with families in mind, it opens its doors to 5000 people a year. A third centre was opened on Exmoor, and now all three are administered (since 1994) by the Calvert Trust. The contact phone number is 01434 250232.

Key to symbols

1 **2** Places mentioned in text	Route of walk (Long Distance)
23 Linear walk mileage	Alternative routes
Woodland	Return routes
Built-up areas	Car Parking
Steep slope	Individual building
Main (A) Roads	Railway line
B Roads	Tracks (metalled in urban areas)
C Roads	Dismantled North Tyne Railway
Path - where it is quite clear on the ground. Otherwise the route arrow shows the general direction of the right of way.	**WM** Waymark (where it is not on a gate or fence post)
Field boundaries (only shown when necessary for route finding)	
Kissing gate	
Gate	
Stile	
Gate across road	
Steps	
Bridge	
CG Cattle Grid	

Walk 1: Hexham to Acomb (Circular)

You might like to visit Hexham Abbey (2), before you start – or on your return. Built mainly in the 12/13th Centuries, its crypt – a must to visit – dates from 674AD, when St. Wilfred built the first church on this site. Also worth a visit are the Moot Hall and the 14th Century Old Gaol (3). Once across the river the walk follows the 'old' road to Acomb before you cross the A69. Acomb has a pretty Main Street. You return past St. John Lee Church (4).

Distance: 4 miles (6km)
Time: 2 hours

Terrain: *Mostly roads, woodland and field paths, 2 kissing gates, 4 other gates. 1 stile.*

Parking: *Wentworth (Hexham)*

Refreshments: *Large number of cafes, restaurants, hotels, pubs in Hexham. Sun Inn, Queens Arms and Miners Arms in Acomb, also fish and chip shop.*

Start: Hexham Market Place (1)

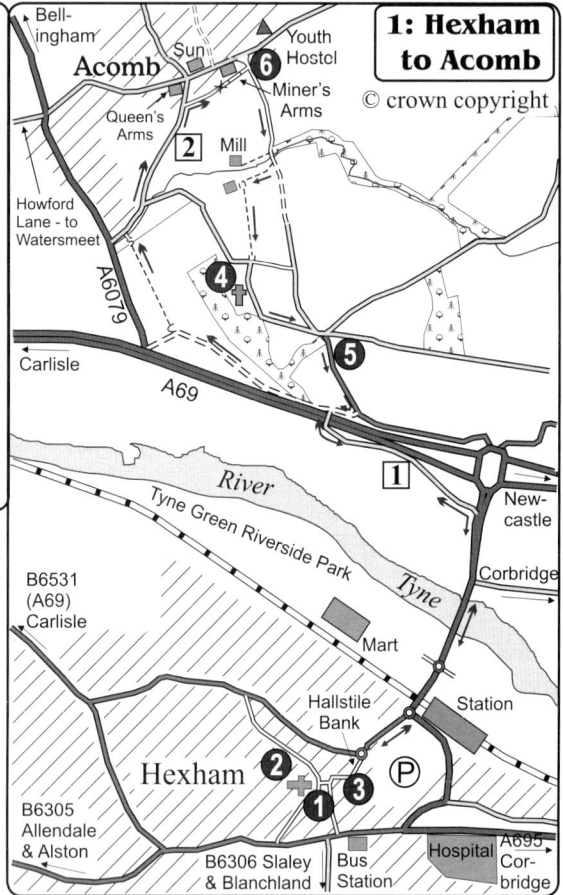

1: Hexham to Acomb

© crown copyright

Go past the Forum Cinema, down Hallstile Bank, and right at the roundabout. Cross the road (pelican crossing) and continue ahead over the railway and then across the bridge over the Tyne. To the East side of the bridge, almost under it, is a weir, where salmon leap on their way upstream. As you approach the A69 roundabout, just before the brown "Kielder water and Forest / Hadrian's Wall" sign turn left and follow the former main road to Bellingham – how narrow it seems! Turn right across the bridge, over the dual carriageway and then left at the signpost "St. John Lee Bridge ½". Continue for just over ¼ mile and after the lane turns left look out for a signpost "Alnmouth Terrace ¼". Turn right, through a kissing gate, and follow a clear field path ending with another kissing gate. Go through this gate and across a footbridge to join Alnmouth Terrace. Follow this uphill, ignoring a road off to your right until you come to a sign post on your right "**Acomb Square ¼"(6)** pointing along a gravelled drive (see below). Long distance walkers continue up the road to Main Street and turn right, just after the Sun Inn, to join Walk 2, which branches off to the left. For Walk 1 take this gravelled drive which turns into a path with a stile and two gates leading into the Square. Turn right and continue down the track to a footbridge. Either take the path on the right just before it and continue beside the stream to the vicinity of the Mill where you take the path uphill to your left or cross the bridge and take the path going uphill above the stream (again on your right). These paths converge at a metal gate, which leads to a field path going straight ahead (with a house on your right) uphill to a gate, leading to a road junction. Take the road leading ahead, to pass **St. John Lee Church (4)** [*The Church takes its name from John of Beverley, a Hexham monk, who founded the earliest church on the site in the 7th Century. There have been churches here ever since. The current one was built in 1843 and much refurbished in 1886. It has a notable wooden ceiling, some medieval stone carvings from its predecessors and a Roman altar for a Font*] Continue along the road to the cottage "**Peaslaw Gates**" **(5)**. Take the right hand one of the five roads that converge here. Where a large tree dominates the next junction, turn right towards the bridge over the A69, which you crossed earlier and retrace your steps across it and back to Hexham.

Walk 2: Acomb to Heavenfield and Wall (Circular)

This attractive walk, mainly on paths and byroads, climbs steadily, but not too arduously up to the site of the battle of Heavenfield, and follows the Hadrian's Wall Path for a short distance before dropping down to the pretty village of Wall 'en route' back to Acomb. Long distance walkers could do the Wall to Acomb stretch in reverse, if pushed for time, thus saving about a mile. See Walk 3 for rather more about Hadrian's Wall. From Planetrees to Wall you can, of course, follow either Walk 2 or Walk 3. I varied the routes only for a slight change of scene!

Distance: 6½ miles (10km) *Time: 3 hours*
Terrain: Country by-roads, field paths, 12 stiles, 9 gates, a few steps.
Parking: Top of Acomb Main Street, in the 'square' though allow space for buses to turn.
Refreshments: Sun Inn, Queens Arms and Miners Arms in Acomb, Fish and Chip shop. Wall - Hadrian Hotel, St. Oswald's Tea Room *(1)* on the Military Road (B6318) – light lunches/teas (summer months)
Start: Acomb 'Square'.

Walk down Main Street past the Miner's Arms and just before the Sun Inn at a signpost "Halfway House ½" turn right into a lane. A wall divides this into two 'lanes', take the right hand one and keep to the left of a house ahead to follow a narrow path, which soon takes you down steps and over a footbridge across the Red Burn. A ladder stile leads into a long field. Follow the left hand edge and look out for another ladder stile to your left. Once over this continue diagonally left, passing close to a house on your left, to a third ladder stile. Turn left into a lane and almost at once right onto the road at Halfway House. Continue uphill for ½ mile until you see a signpost on your right "Written Crag". Go through the gate. The OS map shows the right of way as going straight across the field, but if it is sown, it might be courteous to skirt the Northern edge. Go through the gate on the other side, and across the muddy farm track to Fallowfield, through a gate and turn left at the waymarked post just before Square Wood (don't go through the gate at the edge of the wood). There is no clear path across the field, but aim due North and towards a two-armed signpost, which soon comes into view. To the left of this join the road and turn right and through two gates to reach the Military Road (B6318). [*The road was built by General Wade about the time of the Jacobite Rebellion of 1745 to speed troop movements. Fortunately for him, but unfortunately for posterity, the General pulled down what remained of Hadrian's Wall to provide foundations for his road. For most of the way from Heddon-on-the-Wall to Sewingshields, drivers on the B6318 are riding on top of the wall. This does at least afford Romans' eye views down into the defensive ditch on the North side and wonderful views both North and South*]. Cross the road with care. You might wish to read the information Board beside Heavenfield Cross, commemorating St. Oswald's victory over the pagan Cadwallon in 635 A.D. **St. Oswald's Church (2)**, ahead of you, was rebuilt on the site of earlier churches in 1737. Go through the field gate and turn left to follow Hadrian's Wall Path (for a bit more about the Wall see Walk 3). (If you wish to visit **St. Oswald's Tea Room (1)**, turn right and you will reach it using the path.) Climb over a ladder stile, cross a bumpy field, over a stile, down a steep slope, over another ladder stile. You are now skirting the main road, past Planetrees Farm, which the next stile leads onto. Cross the road (take care), onto a footbridge and down steps into a field. A signpost reads "Fallowfield 1, Brunton ¼". Take the Fallowfield direction slightly left across the field. After a stile over a fence turn left. Skirt the field and cross a ladder stile by a metal gate. Turn right and across a stile into a road. Follow this quiet byroad down to the village of Wall. You have good views across the valley to **Chesters House (6)** (see Walk 3). Turn left to take the road beside the playing field. (There are toilets to your left). Continue along this road, which bears right then left through the village green, until you reach a T-junction. Turn right for the Hadrian Hotel and left to continue this walk up a road, which becomes a farm track after passing "The Vicarage". The track curves right slightly uphill. At a metal gate ahead take the narrower path to the left to reach a metal gate signposted "Public Bridleway ½ mile only then Public Footpath to Fallowfield ¾". A clear path leads across this field towards a gap in gorse bushes between two woods. At this gap you will go through a gate. Keep

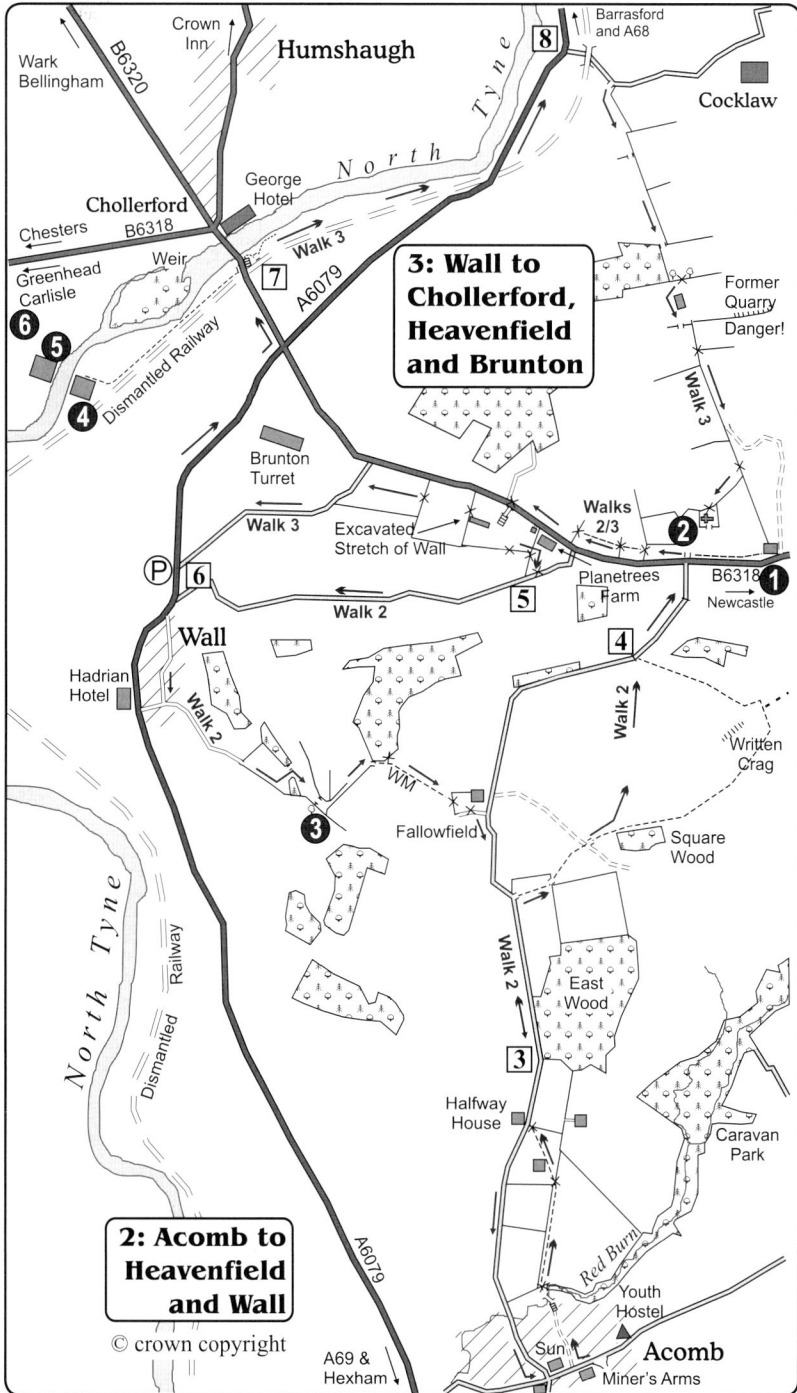

Crown Inn

Humshaugh

Wark Bellingham

B6320

North Tyne

8

Barrasford and A68

Cocklaw

George Hotel

Chollerford

Chesters B6318

Greenhead Carlisle

Weir

Walk 3

7

A6079

Former Quarry Danger!

Walk 3

6

5

4

Dismantled Railway

3: Wall to Chollerford, Heavenfield and Brunton

Brunton Turret

Walk 3

Excavated Stretch of Wall

Walks 2/3

2

Planetrees Farm

B6318

Newcastle

1

(P) **6**

Walk 2

5

Wall

Hadrian Hotel

Walk 2

4

Walk 2

Written Crag

Walk 2

WM

Fallowfield

Square Wood

North Tyne

Dismantled Railway

3

Walk 2

East Wood

3

Halfway House

Caravan Park

2: Acomb to Heavenfield and Wall

© crown copyright

A6079

Red Burn

Youth Hostel

A69 & Hexham

Sun

Acomb

Miner's Arms

right aiming for a few **oak trees (3)**, beyond a metal gate. With walls to your left and right continue up a rocky lane until it leads into a field. Follow the wall on your right. At the edge of the wood ahead of you, beside a Bridleway sign, go through a gate on your right, turn left and follow the edge of the wood for a few yards until you see a stile leading into the wood. Turn your back on this (!) and head diagonally right uphill past a way mark on a post, towards a house behind a small clump of trees. Cross the stone stile ahead, go on through the trees, over another stone stile and turn right onto the road leading to the house. When it shortly meets a farm road turn left into the centre of Fallowfield, and then right at the 'main' road. Follow this down hill into Acomb. Turn left when you reach Main Street and back to your start.

Walk 3: Wall to Chollerford, Heavenfield and Brunton (circular)

This walk contains a variety of scenery. It is our first opportunity to walk along the river-bank and our last to explore part of Hadrian's Wall. After a strenuous climb up from the river the walk passes through St. Oswald's Churchyard (see Walk 2) and follows the line of Hadrian's Wall, before turning off back to Wall. Stout water- and mud-proof boots are advisable.

Distance: 5 miles (8km) *Time*: 2½ hours *(Longer if visiting Chesters)*

Terrain: *Metalled paths, country by-roads, short stretch of main road, but mainly field paths with some muddy stretches. 10 stiles, 6 gates, a few steps*

Parking: *Along the road beside Wall's playing field, where toilets are located, or in lay-by on A6079*

Refreshments: *Wall – Hadrian Hotel, Choller-ford – George Hotel, Humshaugh (pronounced 'Humshalf') – Crown Inn (½ mile from Choller-ford Bridge). St. Oswald's Tea Room (see Walk 2)*

Start: *Wall Village, wherever you have parked*

Note on Hadrian's Wall:

The Romans had explored the North of England ('Britannia') under their General Agricola in the 70's and 80's A.D. Forts were established in the Tyne gap. The Emperor Hadrian, keen to strengthen the frontiers of his Empire, ordered the building of the Wall. This was undertaken between 122 and 128 A.D., by his legions, aided by local labour. Initially the Cumbrian section was a turf wall, but later it, too, was rebuilt in stone. The wall was, to the top of its North-facing rampart, 6 or 7 metres (21 feet) in height. Immediately in front was a deep V-shaped ditch, a serious obstacle for any attacker. Some few hundred yards, but often quite near it, South of the wall was a wide ditch called the vallum, which was bridged at points opposite gateways in the wall itself. This was more of a customs barrier than a line of defence, as threats of actual attack, it was felt, would come from the North. Once they had built the wall the legions retired to form a strategic reserve based at York and Chester. The wall was garrisoned by Auxiliary troops from various parts of the Empire (Syrians may not have relished the climate!). They were housed in 16 forts some 5 or 6 miles apart, between which were Milecastles every Roman mile (The Roman mile - 'Mille Passus' = a 'thousand

The bridge at Chollerford

paces' - each pace was a double step (left! right!) of 5 feet so 1000 of these was 5000 feet. Our modern mile is 5280 feet). These were mini-barracks, with a gateway to the North, where troops may have spent a period of active patrol duty, before returning to the compara- tive comfort of their fort. Between each Milecastle were two turrets, watchtowers, higher than the wall itself. On, or near, Walk 3 you can explore all of these features, except for a Milecastle, as the only one "en route", at Planetrees, has not been excavated.

Head North out of Wall on the path beside the A6079. You might like to visit Brunton Turret and the short section of Hadrian's Wall, which you pass shortly before the A6079/B6318 crossroads. Turn left and, at the Garage, cross the road to keep on a footpath. If you wish to explore more of the wall cross the road and take the well-signposted ½ mile path to the **Roman Bridge abutment (4)** opposite **Chesters Fort (6)**. This is a massive structure, built where the river interrupted the wall itself. You can see the splendidly preserved **Bath House (5)** on the opposite bank. If this further whets your appetite you do have to retrace your steps to the modern road bridge, cross it and continue left beside the B6318 to Chesters Fort (½ mile). To continue Walk 3 take the steps to your right, signposted "Chollerton 1¾", just before the bridge. Go down the steps round to the right and through a gate to reach a path between a field and the river. Follow this until you cross a board walk to enter scrubby woodland with a high retaining wall protecting the road to your right. You soon climb steps to reach the A6079 again, where a sign points back to Chollerford. Turn left along the road. There is no footpath, but a wide grassy verge to avoid passing traffic. After a couple of hundred yards turn right into the byroad to Cocklaw. Long distance walkers should continue along the A6079 (see Link Walk 4). The current walk takes you under the old railway bridge.

[This branch of the old North British Railway, which closed in 1956, linked Hexham and the Tyne Valley with Morpeth and Rothbury via Reedsmouth Junction and the Scottish Border towns and Edinburgh via the remote Riccarton Junction. The railway follows the North Tyne and you will meet it often in the course of these walks. It is worth pondering how much labour went into the cuttings, embankments, bridges and viaducts on even this one relatively little used branch line.]

Where the road bends sharp left turn off right at a metal gate signposted "St. Oswald's Church, Heavenfields 1¼". You enter an often very muddy field and turn left to follow the fence, keeping right and then left to skirt a wall ahead, after which the hedge continues till you reach a metal gate. This leads to a steep climb up a field with a gully on your right and hedge/fence on your left. The ground levels out as you approach a third metal gate with a wood to your right. [For the next few hundred yards the route does not quite accord with the directions shown on the OS Map]. Aim for a point between two trees ahead on your immediate skyline where you will find a stile and your first way mark since leaving the main road. Follow the direction indicated up a muddy, shrub covered slope. After negotiating a dip in the ground, with ruined corrugated iron huts to your left, turn left at a way mark post and continue uphill between two grassy banks to where another way mark guides you slightly left to pass through the stone posts of a former gate way. Continue to a ladder stile ahead of you on the immediate skyline [**Warning note** – The fence which runs East of the stone pillared gateway is the boundary of a former quarry whose steep wall you will have noticed to your left on your way uphill. Should you wish to do this walk in reverse **on no account climb over that fence** which guards a concealed sheer drop]. Follow the field boundary to your right, go through a gateway, but keep along the field edge, avoiding the farm track curving away ahead of you. You will see a small brick building in rather marshy ground. Opposite this, on your right, is the stile, followed by a footbridge, which you cross to continue uphill to St. Oswald's Church. Aim for the left of the building and you will come to a stone stile leading into the Churchyard, which you leave through a gate and across a field to the main road. (See note on Heavenfield in Walk 2). Turn right at the gate leading to the road following the Hadrian's Wall path signs (i.e. Stay in the field). (To visit St. Oswald's Tearoom follow the path signs to your left - East - a 5 minute walk at most). To continue this walk, the path uses a ladder stile to reach a bumpy field. A stile then leads to a steep downward slope. Another ladder stile brings you to a field beside the B6318. Follow the field edge to a stile, which brings you onto the road. Cross with care to a footbridge leading to steps. Turn right at the signpost "Fallowfield 1, Brunton ¼". "¼" is wishful thinking as Brunton Turret is at least a mile further on, but perhaps flagging Path walkers needed encouragement! You will pass the Planetrees length of wall – sadly the adjacent Milecastle has not been excavated. If you wish to get an idea of what the Vallum looked like, turn left just before the ladder stile you are due to cross and walk a few yards along the field edge. The big gully stretching uphill is **not** the Vallum, but a few yards further on you will see that it is quite clearly a man-made depression leading uphill, and you get a good idea of its width and depth. Return to the ladder stile and as you are on the line of the wall, you can see an impressive stretch of V ditch on your right – the ditch at Planetrees has disappeared over the years. Another ladder stile brings you into a strip of woodland. You emerge at a road junction. Take the byroad – left – past Middle Brunton and down to the A6079. Turn left to return to Wall.

Walk 4: Cocklaw Road to Barrasford (Linear)

Distance (one-way): 1¾ miles (3km)
Time: ¾ hour

Terrain: Roads, Field/woodland paths, very steep indeed in two places, 5 stiles (3 on alternative route), 2 gates

Refreshments: Barrasford Arms (3)

Parking: On the wide grassy verge on the by-road (off A 6079) to **Cocklaw (1)**. Take care to leave enough room for wide farm vehicles which may overlap the narrow road, to pass.

Start: Your parking place, unless of course walking from Hexham or Wall

I have not discovered a feasible circular walk to follow Walk 3, without over-long stretches on the busy A 6079. So this short section links Walks 3 and 5, for those wanting to walk, for example, the 10 miles from Wall to Wark. It is a pleasant stroll to Barrasford and back in its own right, but a couple of very steep slopes would be difficult in icy, or wet conditions. The descent through the woods is extremely over-grown in summer and can be very slippery in adverse weather conditions (see note on page 16). It can be very tough indeed to follow the 'path' in the top section. The woods here, once entirely Elm, which has since gone, contain some 'taxing' vegetation.

Walk back to the A6079 and turn right. There is no footpath beside this busy stretch of the main road, so take care. Note the beautifully built skewed railway bridge as you pass beneath it. At Chollerton Church turn left into the quieter Barrasford road, still no pavement unfortunately. After about ½ mile where the road had just curved to the right look out for a signpost "Barrasford ¾" by a stile on your left. Cross a short stretch of field to a gate and descend into the railway cutting. Do not follow what seems the obvious route along the railway, but take the path going up the opposite side of the cutting. This path descends steeply to a stile, leading to a rough boggy field. Follow the path along the right-hand side of the field with woods on your right past a way marked post

15

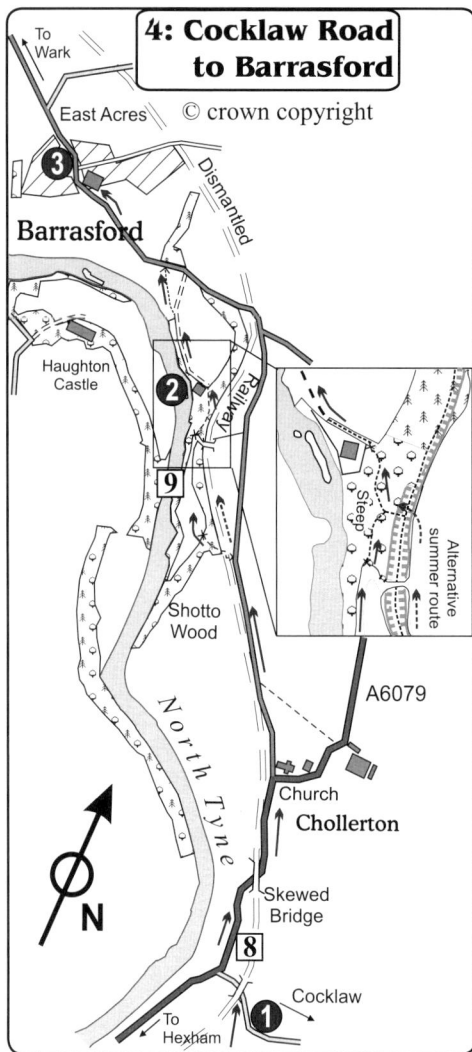

4: Cocklaw Road to Barrasford

© crown copyright

To Wark

East Acres

Dismantled

Barrasford

Railway

Haughton Castle

Shotto Wood

North Tyne

N

Steep

Alternative summer route

A6079

Church

Chollerton

Skewed Bridge

Cocklaw

To Hexham

and climb uphill until you come to a stile over a fence. You enter woods and for a short distance the path is narrow, wandering along the top of a precipitous slope down to the river. When the path curves right back to the railway cutting, turn sharp left and again very steeply downhill, to a large building (pumping station?) protected by a beech hedge.

Note: In summer months you can avoid the initial descent to the field as it is very over-grown. Instead stay on the railway line, although it should be emphasised that this is not a right of way. After ¼ mile you pass under an old railway bridge and 100 yards beyond, a path leads to the left out of the cutting, level with a fallen tree. After a short distance fork right down hill to rejoin the route.

The path continues over a stile and round the right hand edge of the building between the hedge and a fence to a metal gate. Turn right along the unmade up road with the river below you to your left. A line of telegraph poles support a lone wire beside the road. Between the 3rd and 4th posts turn off left keeping a lone tree to your right. The path continues along a grassy ledge to a stile (signposted whence you have come "Chollerton 1¼"). Turn left onto the road and follow it with care (no footpath) into Barrasford village. Just after the **Barrasford Arms (3)**, a road leads off right (opposite a Public Telephone) to the village school and East Acre. I suggest that you park anywhere convenient along this road for Walk 5, which you can now join by continuing along the main road.

Spare a moment to look across the river to your left at the imposing Haughton Castle (see Walk 6) dominating the opposite bank.

Walk 5: Barrasford to Gunnerton, Toddle Crag and Cat's Elbow (Circular)

An undemanding (though boggy in some places), but interesting walk along the crags, which encircle the extensive Barrasford Quarry. Apart from a short stretch past the actual quarry works, the quarry itself is hidden behind rugged and attractive countryside. Although the OS map suggests a diversion to Swinburne Castle, this is in fact private property without public access.

Distance: 4½ miles (7 km) Time : 2 hours

Terrain: Roads, metalled paths, unmade up farm roads, field paths, 2 stiles, 11 gates

Parking: In Barrasford on the road leading to the school (1) *and East Acre.*

Refreshments: Barrasford Arms (2)

Start: *Where you have parked in Barrasford*

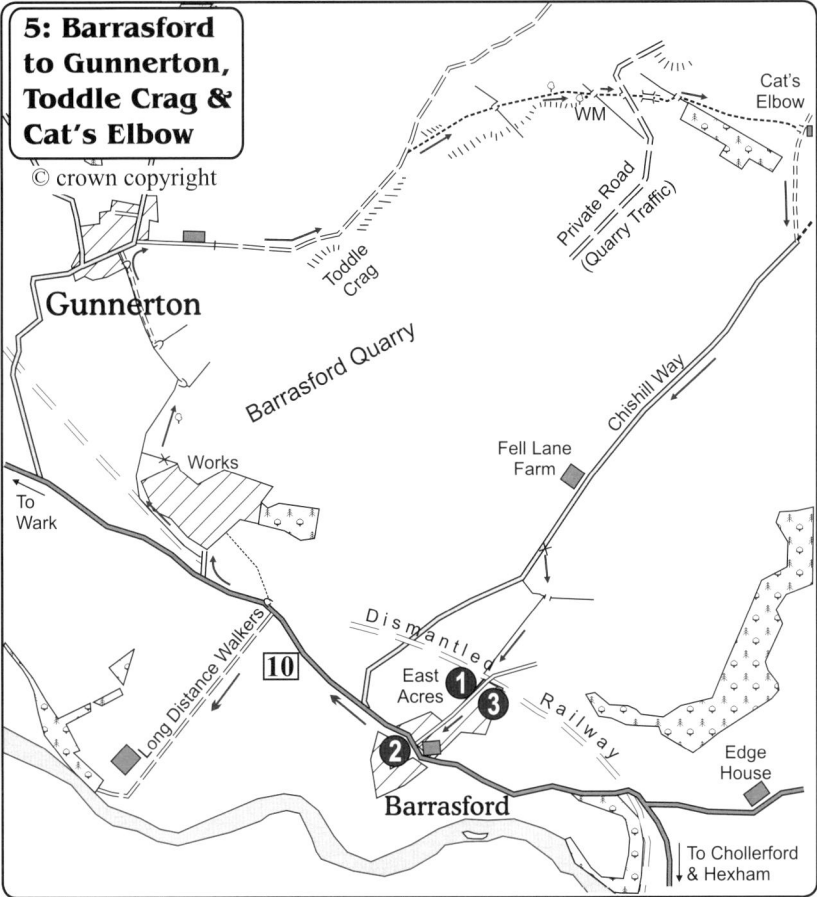

5: Barrasford to Gunnerton, Toddle Crag & Cat's Elbow

© crown copyright

Rejoin the main road from Hexham turn right and cross it, re-crossing to the right hand side when the pavement runs out. Continue along the footpath until, where the road bends left, a signpost on the far side indicates a Public Bridleway, which is in fact the long straight metalled road to Riverhill Farm. Long distance walkers should turn down this road and turn to Walk 6 for map and directions. On your right at this point is a kissing gate signposted "Gunnerton 1". Ignore this and continue beside the road to the quarry entrance ("Tarmac"). Turn right and having passed the metal gate and twin black and yellow posts turn left as indicated by a way mark. Continue beside the fence to your right passing to the left of a metal gate. Follow the fence where it soon turns sharp right and left. A footbridge and ladder stile are provided, but the path now bypasses both. Continue along the now narrow path with a fence on your left and a wooded bank on you right, which the path moves onto as it curves right beside the quarry perimeter fence. Where fences merge to block your way, cross a ladder stile into a field and head across this to a kissing gate in a wall. Turn left to follow the far side of this wall, which becomes a fence, go through another gate and along the edge of the next field to a third kissing gate and into a short lane leading to the road, which weaves its way through Gunnerton. Turn right. After a few yards at a signpost "Gunnerton Nick ½, Great Swinburne 2¼" turn right along an unmetalled road, which, after a gate, curves round below the impressive Toddle Crag. Just after this a wide grassy track curves off uphill to the right, follow this up and round to the left, above a line of low cliffs to a gate. The path narrows but is still easy to follow with a rock-strewn slope on the right. You continue through scrub and hawthorn over a gully. You need to be sure-footed hereabouts as the path traverses a slope below a low crag. It soon opens out into more level going to reach a waymarked post. Ignore the direction shown here and continue slightly left to a gate, which leads down to the new road, put in for the quarry wagons and only shown on the most recent OS maps. Cross it at the gravel ramps on either side. Go across a footbridge, through a gate and bear right, then left on a wide grassy path up a slope. Go through

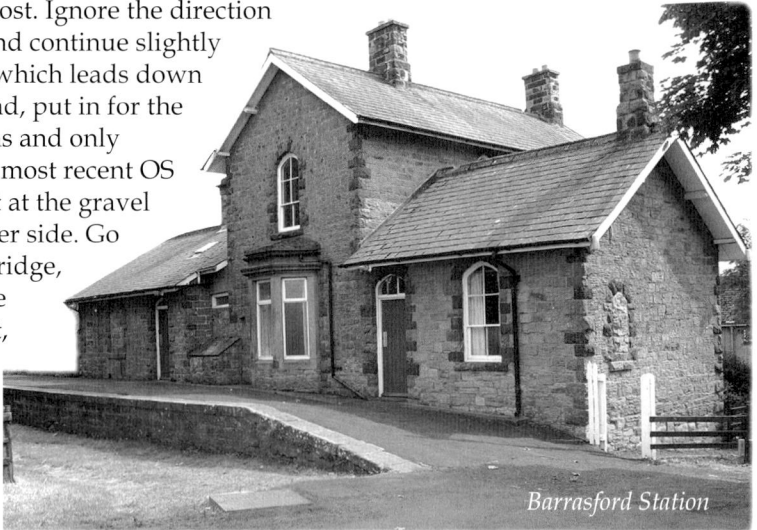

Barrasford Station

a gate, with a wood on your right. At the far side of the boggy, tussocky field you now cross is a cottage, 'Cat's Elbow'. Aim for its left hand end and emerge through a gate onto a metalled lane, (a signpost points back, whence you have come to "Gunnerton 1½"). Turn right along this lane – Chishill Way. After a mile you reach Fell Lane Farm. Look out for a signpost "East Acres ¼" on your left a short distance after the farm. Cross a stile, turn right then slightly left to the far side of a field. Ignore a gate immediately ahead but continue to the left to a waymarked metal gate. This leads to a field where you follow the fence and hedge on its right hand edge, turn left round the far edge and shortly right to cross the old railway trackbed at the charming **station (3)**, hardly changed, externally, since it closed to passengers in 1956. You are now at East Acres, so follow the road past the school (why "Chollerton" school, I wondered, since it is in Barrasford?) to your car.

Walk 6: Gunnerton to Chipchase (circular)

A very pleasant walk with no difficult sections, providing good riverside stretches and wide-ranging views of the North Tyne valley. Views too of Haughton and Chipchase Castles. Although I would strongly recommend doing the whole walk, it can be shortened (B) or split into two separate short walks (C and D). The text and map explain the alternatives.

Distances: 7½ miles (12km) Time: 3½ hours (for the full walk)

Terrain: Roads, unmetalled farm road, field paths. One stream to cross on unstable stepping stones, 7 stiles, 7 gates (more, or less, on the alternatives – see map)

Parking: In West Crescent, Gunnerton (1). This is a residential road, so please take care not to cause an obstruction

Refreshments: Nearest are at Barrrasford (Walk 5) and Wark (Walk 7)

Start: From West Crescent

The directions that follow show where the routes of the four alternative walks A, B, C and D merge or separate. The map shows the appropriate letters as a backup. All four walks turn right out of West Crescent onto the main road. Shortly after it bends right, at a signpost "Barrasford 1½" A, B and C turn left down a short lane. [D continues through the village round left and right bends to where the road curves left to the old railway bridge and a short unmetalled lane signposted "Burnmouth Cottages ½" leads to a stile beside a metal gate. Beyond these the path goes slightly to the right across a field to the main road. At the gate signposted back to "Gunnerton ½" at the main road, turn right to rejoin walks A and B]. Back in Gunnerton (!), A, B and C continue through a kissing gate beside a metal gate, along a very muddy tractor track with a fence on your right which becomes a wall after you have passed another kissing gate and a metal gate. Continue along the field edge to a third kissing gate, waymarked for you to turn right.

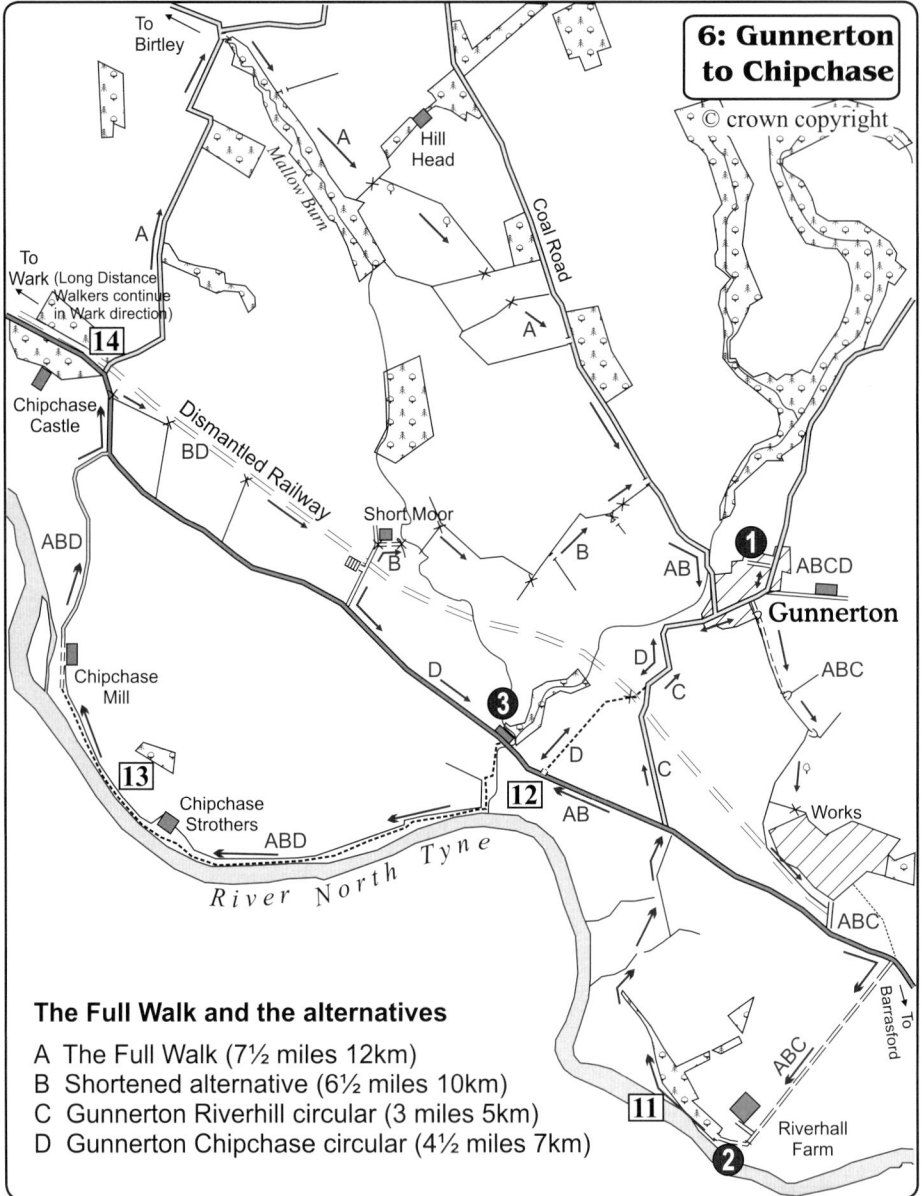

© crown copyright

To Birtley

Hill Head

Mallow Burn

Coal Road

To Wark (Long Distance Walkers continue in Wark direction)

14

Chipchase Castle

Dismantled Railway

BD

Short Moor

ABD

Chipchase Mill

13

Chipchase Strothers

ABD

3

D

D

12

AB

B

AB

1

ABCD

Gunnerton

ABC

C

C

D

Works

ABC

River North Tyne

To Barrasford

ABC

11

Riverhall Farm

2

The Full Walk and the alternatives

A The Full Walk (7½ miles 12km)
B Shortened alternative (6½ miles 10km)
C Gunnerton Riverhill circular (3 miles 5km)
D Gunnerton Chipchase circular (4½ miles 7km)

Continue along a grassy ledge with a lone tree to your left and a wall a little way off on your right to a ladder stile. Cross this and shortly follow the path, which curves off right then left beside the perimeter fence of Barrasford quarry. You turn right and then left at a redundant ladder stile and footbridge to join a metalled road which leads you out of the works entrance to the main road.

20

Turn left along the footpath, and shortly cross the road where a not very informative signpost (it merely says "footpath") points you onto the straight, metalled, lane to Riverhill Farm. As you walk along this lane you get a good view to your left of Haughton Castle.

[*Built c1268 probably by William de Swyneburn, treasurer to Alexander III of Scotland – the Anglo-Scottish border being, then, ill defined. Ransacked by Mosstroopers from Liddlesdale in 1542, it remained an empty shell until restored and modernised internally in 17th/18th Centuries. In 1816 Haughton village was razed to the ground and the villagers removed to Humshaugh – to improve the view from the castle!*]

Keep straight on where the lane veers right to the farm and an unmetalled road leads you through a metal gate and curves right to approach the river at a **Gauging Station (2)** (A Gauging Station measures the water flow in a river. There are about 5 along the length of the North Tyne). Shortly after this go through a gate and follow the track as it curves away from the river with oak trees climbing up on your right. Where these end the track curves left past a "strictly private" sign. A home-made wooden sign points you to the right and the path continues somewhat unclearly through tussocky grass to a waymarked footbridge. Instead of crossing it, continue up the edge of the field with a hedge and ditch on your left until a wide gap beckons you to your left. Accept this invitation although there is no waymark. Bear slightly right following a wide track across a field to another gap where another ditch nearly meets a wall. Here there is a waymark. Go through the gap and up the field with the wall in your right to the main road at a signpost pointing back to "Riverhill Farm ¾" (Those doing Walk C should cross the road and follow the side road signposted to Gunnerton back through the village to West Crescent). A and B walkers turn left and continue along the main road (take care as there is no footpath) and are soon joined by D walkers emerging from the gate signposted "Gunnerton ½". The road then descends to a bridge, just before which a signpost "Chipchase Mill 1¼" indicates a path off to the left. Unfortunately when I explored the ford to which this leads I had to go in well over my boots and then slipped on uneven stones up to my knees, so returned to the road, on which you should continue over the bridge to **Burnmouth Cottages (3)**. Opposite on your left is a wide gateway labelled "Keep dogs in a lead". Until you rejoin the Right of Way as you approach the river bank a short distance beyond this, the Chipchase Estate have very kindly granted permissive path status to the wide grassy track that you now follow through the gate over the brow of a small hill. As it descends it becomes a tractor track and curves right and then left beside a fence on your right, with a plantation of young trees on your left. The path soon curves right to follow the river bank on a wide easy track past Chipchase Strothers to Chipchase Mill where it becomes a metalled road and a signpost tells you that you have walked 1½ miles from Burnmouth Cottages and 2 from Gunnerton though A and B walkers have done double those

Chipchase Castle

distances. As you continue up to the main road, the imposing Chipchase Castle comes into view.

[*Chipchase Castle incorporates three distinct building periods. The West Tower was built by the Heron family, of Ford Castle in North Northumberland, in 1348. This is now an adjunct of the 1621 Manor House said to be the finest example in the country of Jacobean architecture. A Georgian wing was added in 1784. Both Haughton and Chipchase are private residences, open only on special occasions, though Chipchase Castle Nursery is open to the public in the Summer*].

Turn left onto the main road. After about 100 yards a signpost at a stile by two metal gates points to "Gunnerton 1¾". B and D walkers should cross this stile and follow directions given below. Meanwhile the stalwart A walkers continue a few yards to the road junction and turn right (for Birtley and Woodburn). Long distance walkers continue left along the main road and should now turn to Walk 7. Walk 6 continues up this pleasant side road. After just short of a mile where the road dips down to a junction with Birtley a mile off to the left, go through the metal gate on your right merely signposted 'Footpath' and continue with a fence on your right beyond another gate and skirt to the left of a clump of trees and keep leftish across the field, with Hill Head further up on your left, to a waymarked stile. Continue across the next boggy field keeping to the right of two lone trees, and some distance from the fence on your left. You pass what looks like a small milestone with 'M' carved on it, near some manholes (water main?), to a waymarked stile. The waymark points you diagonally left across two fields separated by a stile to join the Coal Road. If these fields are sown, it might be more sensible to turn left along the grassy verge on the left and follow it round right through a gateway to join the road at that point. Either way, turn right and follow the road into Gunnerton village. Turn left at the T-junction and back to West Crescent.

B and D walkers who have been waiting patiently at the stile by the two metal gates at Chipchase continue along the fence on your right, bypass a redundant stile, and follow along beside the railway embankment over two more stiles to the railway bridge which you reach by climbing steps to a gate. Turn right for Walk D, left for B. Incidentally the going along the fields beside the railway is quite heavy so you might be tempted to use the unofficial, but apparently well-worn track along the railway itself, but I stress the word 'tempted'. To complete Walk D, go down to the main road, turn left, and once past Burnmouth Cottages just retrace your steps along the outward route of D. Back on Walk B, just after the railway bridge and just before Short Moor look out for a stile almost hidden in the hedge on your right. Cross it and continue beside the garden wall (on your left) and down a slope with a fence now beside you to a stile, which leads to a ford over the Mallow Burn, which is fordable, but slippery. Continue uphill almost to the corner of the field where there is a stile over a fence on your right. Continue along the hedgerow (with only vestiges of the hedge remaining) at the top of this field to a stile after which turn left. This field is boggy. Go through a metal gate, then over a stile beside another metal gate, then left over a stile and follow the field edge (on your right) down through a gateway onto the Coal Road. Turn right and continue into Gunnerton village, left at the T-junction and back to West Crescent.

Walk 7: Wark to Birtley Church and Parkhouse Wood (circular)

This is a very pretty walk climbing up from the North Tyne to Birtley and back down through fields and woodland to a final mile on road. It is probably best as a summer walk as some stretches can be slippery and difficult in very wet weather. Long distance walkers coming through from Chipchase join the final stretch of this walk.

If you have parked in Wark Village, cross the river on Wark Bridge and turn left; if you parked on this side of the river continue along this road towards Birtley.

Distance: 4 miles (7 km) Time: 2 hours

Terrain: Road, field and woodland paths, Some shallow fords, 3 stiles, 5 gates

Parking: Street parking in Wark village or turn left after crossing Wark Bridge from the village and park on the verge – room for 8 cars (3).

Refreshments: Wark – Battlesteads Hotel (1), Grey Bull (2) and Black Bull (2), Birtley – The Percy Arms (open evenings 8-11pm, walking groups can request midday opening – phone 01434 230696

Start: East end of Wark Bridge (3)

[Wark has a long history, being dominated from Norman times by a castle, probably on the site of the mound on your right as you drive into the village from the South. The village was under Scottish rule between 1139 and 1295. It was the acknowledged capital of North Tynedale and justice was dispensed from the Castle. St. Michael's Church, on the Bellingham Road, ¼ mile out of the village, is notable for its Altar Cross, which was originally given to Buckingham Palace's Chapel by Tsar Nicholas II, but subsequently by King George V to St. Michael's.]

The road bears right and up a hill to a junction. Follow the road, signposted "Birtley 1" up over the railway bridge and, not long after a side road off to the right leading down to the former Wark Station, look out for a signpost on your left to "Birtley ½". Go through the metal gate beside it, turn right and follow an indistinct but wide pathway, which gradually diverges from the road to the left hand end of a wood, crossing a ditch en route. As you skirt the wood the path becomes clearer and soon descends a steep slope to cross a stream on a plank, and then a waymarked stile. The path now follows a fence steeply uphill until you are confronted by a walled garden. Follow the wall left to a stile, which leads to a path, fenced on either side, taking you through a V-shaped stile to the road, almost opposite St. Giles Church. Turn right down the road and very soon left down a side road. Where this turns slightly left uphill you will see a two-armed signpost ("Public Footpath and Public Bridleway") on your right. Follow the latter direction towards a fence running along the field side on your left. Ignore a stile over a fence, but go through a waymarked gateway and continue with the fence now on your right. A footbridge and waymarked gate leads you into Parkhouse Wood. The path at first skirts the fence and wall at the edge of the wood, with the steep valley of Dinley Burn on your right. The path is boggy in places but then it broadens and swings further into the wood before bending left to bring you out onto the tarmac roadway in Parkhouse Farm. Continue ahead then right along the road to a cattle grid. Turn off the road onto grass to the right beside a wall to a waymarked gate at the edge of trees. Continue a few yards ahead to a wide gateway leading into a wood and flanked by a telegraph pole encouragingly labelled '**Danger of Death**'. Don't enter the wood (or climb the pole!). Instead turn left following a wide zigzag track steeply downhill past a waymarked post to a dilapidated gateway to your right. It is tempting then to follow the track round to your right, where some white posts seem to suggest a trail, but don't and as this path veers right, cross a rather battered moss-covered ford to your left. Ignore a wide path leading up from it further into the woods but turn right towards a broken bridge over another stream. The bridge is unsafe so you must cross the stream by another ford, which needs care – and probably a skilfully aimed jump – to cross if the stream is higher than usual. Follow the remnants of a fence uphill on your left and near the top as Comogan Farm buildings come clearly into view go through the fence and round bushes up to the top of the wood to the left of the farm where you meet a wall. Continue along beside this and round right to join the farm road and follow it down to the main road where long distance walkers join the walk. Turn right and follow it back to Wark Bridge. Incidentally, if you were hoping for a well-deserved drink at the 'Inn' marked on the OS map at the end of Wark Station road, you will have to wait until you reach the village as that 'Inn' is now a private house.

8: Wark - Heugh & Birtley

© crown copyright

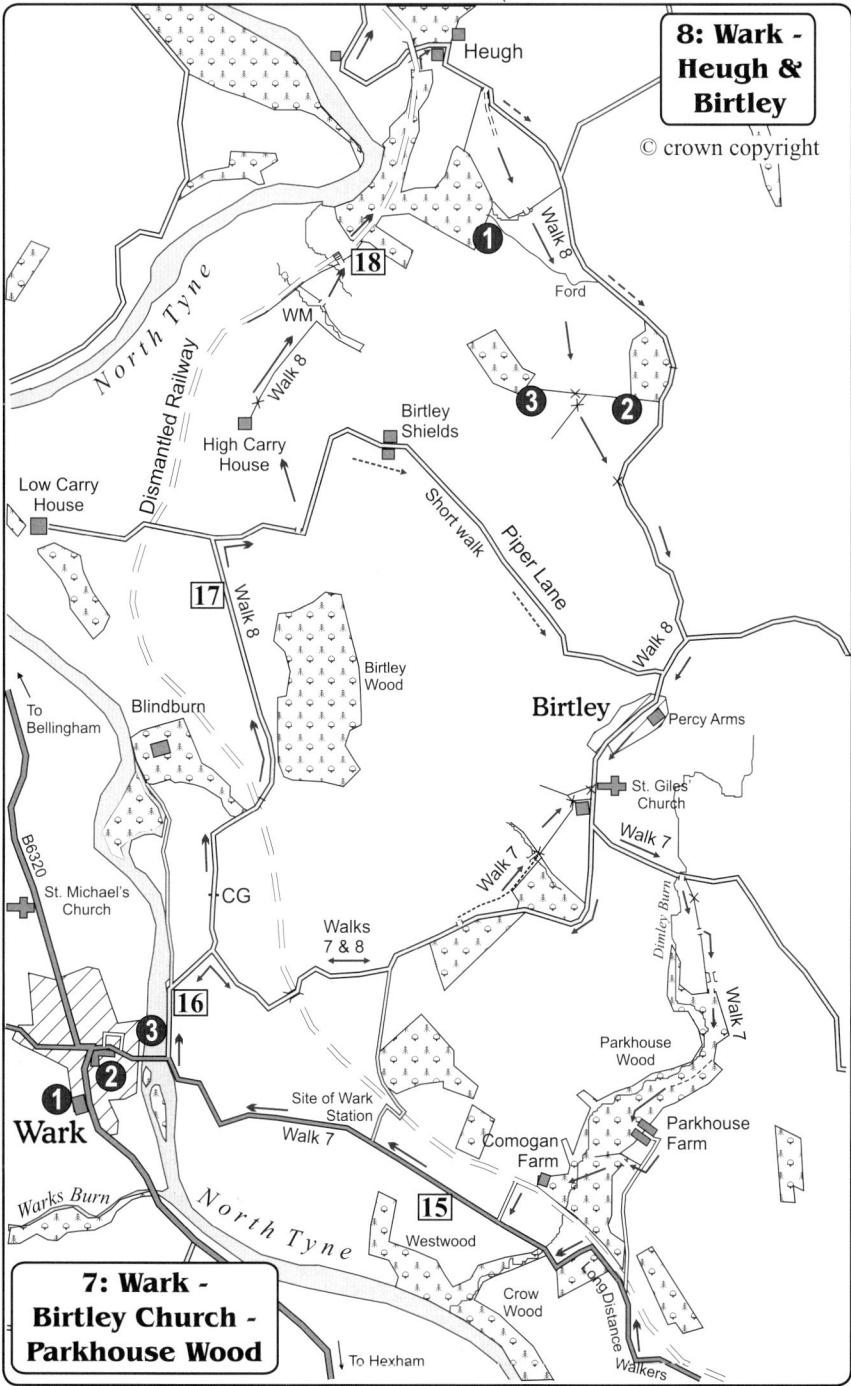

Heugh

Walk 8

18

Ford

WM

Walk 8

2

3

Birtley Shields

High Carry House

Low Carry House

Short walk

Piper Lane

North Tyne

Dismantled Railway

17

Walk 8

Birtley Wood

Walk 8

Blindburn

Birtley

Percy Arms

To Bellingham

St. Giles Church

B6320

Walk 7

Walk 7

St. Michael's Church

CG

Walk 7

Dimley Burn

Walks 7 & 8

Walk 7

16

Parkhouse Wood

3

2

Site of Wark Station

Parkhouse Farm

1

Wark

Walk 7

Comogan Farm

Warks Burn

North Tyne

15

Westwood

Long Distance Walkers

7: Wark - Birtley Church - Parkhouse Wood

Crow Wood

To Hexham

Upper North Tynedale - From Wark (pronounced as in 'Ark') you are in Reiver country, whence both Northwards and Southwards those hardy brigands, the Border Reivers, rode out to steal cattle and terrorize their more peaceable neighbours. Their descendents, Charltons, Robsons, Milburns, Armstrongs and Elliots are still familiar Border names. Those wild times produced a unique form of defensive architecture the Pele Tower (from Latin "pilum" – a javelin) and the Bastle (from the French "bastille"), both solid, squat double storied defensive structures of rough-hewn stone blocks. Livestock would be driven into the ground floor while the family's access to the upper level was by an internal ladder, easily pulled up when enemy approached. The best of these 16th century bastles are at Hole (see Walk 10 map), and at Gatehouse and Black Middens some 2 miles North of Greenhaugh (see Walks 12 and 13) on the Comb road.

The remains of the Mottes at Wark and Tarset remind us that these castles were a feature of the 13th and 14th century struggles over this disputed border land where Scottish rule prevailed for a time. The Romans were here too of course, and an Iron Age settlement is preserved at Tower Knowe on the shores of Kielder Water (Walk 16 map).

To find out more about North Tynedale do visit the Heritage Centre in the Old Station Yard at Bellingham (open Easter to end of October – 10:30 am to 4:30 pm daily except Tuesdays and Wednesdays). It houses a range of excellent and imaginative exhibitions, with a host of evocative artefacts.

Walk 8: Wark to Heugh and Birtley (circular)

This is an interesting and attractive walk, mainly along little used roads, but with one (or two if you wish) quite rugged cross-country stretches and a section along the disused railway line. The return leg affords some wonderful views, from Cheviot in the North to Cross Fell in the South West. The shorter, all road, alternative is a splendid all year round walk, to be done, if possible on a day when maximum winter or summer visibility can be had.

Distance: 6 miles (9 km) Time: 3 hrs

Terrain: Country roads, firm railway track bed, fields and some marshy moorland. Several narrow streams to ford, 1 or 4 stiles, 7 or 8* gates, short flight of steps*

Parking: As for Walk 7

Refreshments: As for Walk 7

Start: As for Walk 7

* depends on route on return leg

Start off as for Walk 7 from your parking place, but at the road junction for Birtley, turn left ("Low Carry House 1½") and follow the road for a mile through 2 gates (the first at a cattle grid) and past Birtley Wood, much of which had been felled when I reconnoitred this walk at the end of 2004. Where the Low Carry House road turns off left, continue sharp right (signpost "High Carry House/Redesmouth") along the road to the next sharp bend (to the left) where another signpost opposite two metal gates beckons you left through a gate to "High Carry house ¼ Redesmouth ½ [If you wish only to do the short all road walk then stay on the road, follow it up to and past Birtley Shields and back along Piper Lane (from which you can get those wonderful views on a clear day) to Birtley and the last mile and a half of this walk]. To continue Walk 8 aim for the old Bastle Tower at High Carry House keeping the rock-strewn slope, and marshy stream below it, to your left until you can find a dryish spot to cross the latter. Cross the ladder stile immediately to the right of the buildings and turn sharp right to follow a wall and electric fence with a steep slope on your left. The wall becomes a fence and where this turns right, you will see a waymark on a hawthorn tree just below you on the left. Follow the direction shown down across a stream to a metal gate in a fence. Go leftish across the next field, past another hawthorn to a gate in a wall leading to steps down to the dismantled railway bed. Although the OS map shows the path continuing up steps and over a stile to the river, parts of it have eroded so our walk continues right along the railway until you turn right, just before a bridge over a road, and descend through a green metal gate to that road. [Long distance walkers turn left and join Walk 9 under the railway bridge.] Turn right up the hill through Heugh Farm. Look out for a signpost "Birtley 1½" on your right, which gives you the choice of taking that path across country or continuing up the road, which the path rejoins a mile further on. The road is the better option for wide ranging views and the path is not recommended on the sort of wet soggy midwinter's day on which my wife and I tried it out – a robust walk from the outset, as we couldn't open the gate at the start so had to climb it. Follow the rutted track uphill, and when it peters out head towards the left-hand edge of a line of three trees, leading down to the currently (2005) **felled wood to the right (1)**. Go through the gate in the fence at the trees. Follow a faint track uphill to a ford over a stream at the next sparse line of trees. Go slightly right, then left through a gap in an earth dyke – all this area appears to have been some sort of old field system with criss-crossing drainage channels and low dykes. It is marshy and crossing the various watercourses involves careful choice of footholds. Your general direction (as waymarks are few and far between) should be between **woods (2) and (3)** on the map, but as a long row of low trees appear on the skyline almost ¼ mile ahead aim for the 4 taller trees in the centre. This should bring you to a couple of ladder stiles in the corner of a walled field. On the second of these is, at last, a clear waymark, which directs up to the Birtley road, though one final watery ditch will tax your fording skills, before you cross the stile and turn right for Birtley. As you enter the village you turn right onto the main road and follow this downhill, ignoring two side roads off to the left, unless you want to take the second one to inspect the now disused Wark Station, whose platforms and station buildings remain in situ. Continue down to the main road and turn right to Wark village. Otherwise continue down the Birtley – Wark road and turn left at signpost "Wark ½" to the village and/or your car.

Walk 9: Heugh to Redesmouth (circular)

This walk takes you through Countesspark Wood following close to the Tyne to Redesmouth – the 'Clapham Junction' of the old North British Railway – and back mainly through fields, with one quite steep climb, to the start with Buteland Farm as the only large dwelling on the return leg and excellent views up and down the Tyne Valley. If the going for any reason – frost, excessive rain – is inimicable to the field paths you will see from the map that the road, mostly little used by vehicles, is an alternative. Though a bit longer, it is in fact no slower as you can keep up a rather faster pace on the firm footing.

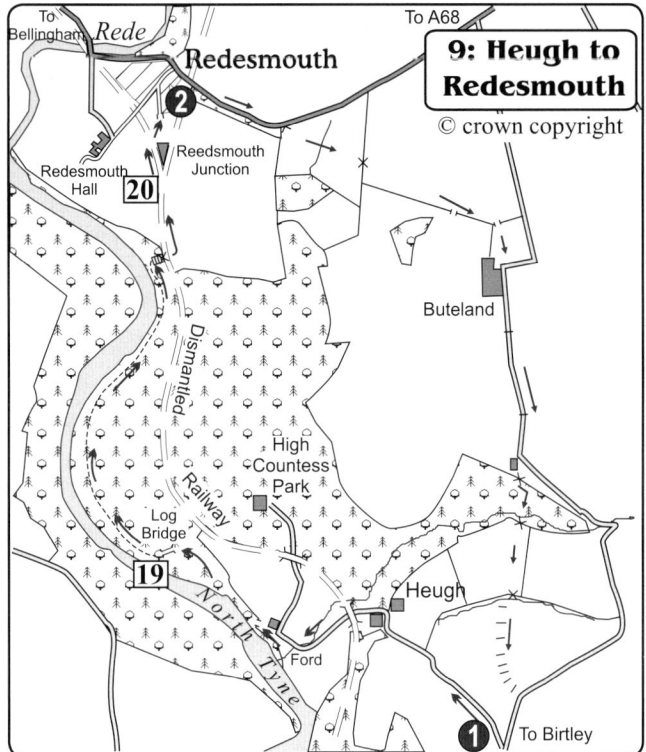

9: Heugh to Redesmouth

© crown copyright

Go down the road to Heugh, through the farm, under the railway bridge (beneath which is a metal gate), over a shallow ford where the road curves right to a house overlooking the river. A waymark guides you left off the road in front of this house. You soon come to a gate and enter Countesspark Wood.

Distance: 4½ miles (7 km) *Time*: 2 hours

Terrain: A mixture of road, firm woodland path, and wet marshy/muddy in places moorland, 5 stiles, 5 gates and a flight of steps

Parking: On verges at (1) (Junction Heugh/Buteland roads) but road becomes dangerous in icy conditions and the verge unstable when very wet so do the circle to/from Redesmouth, where you can street park, if either of those conditions prevail

Refreshments: None on this walk, but Percy Arms, Birtley is 1 mile to the south and for Bellingham (2½ miles from Redesmouth) – see Walk 10

Start: Where you have parked, if this is in Redesmouth I suggest the wide lane by the bungalows (2), but please take care not to obstruct private entrances

28

A clear path leads you to a log 'bridge' over a stream and becomes a broad trail, following the line of the river. After a riverside log cabin the path narrows and becomes muddy in places until you reach steps leading up to the railway, which you reach via a stile. Turn left and follow the track bed to Redesmouth. As you approach the old station the path becomes extremely muddy, as cattle inhabit this stretch.

[*The station is Reedsmouth Junction, the railway using the local spelling, which was in use when it was built in 1861. Trains from Hexham to the Scottish border took the left fork, while a local service to and from Scotsgap for Morpeth and Rothbury terminated at the other platform. The latter service provided 2 or 3 trains a day and the Hexham line 4 or 5, so it is not surprising that passenger services had ceased by 1956 and goods trains by 1963. At its peak though this was quite a substantial railway 'hub' and you can still see the lofty signalbox – now a private house – the engine shed, where English and Scottish crews changed over and of course the station itself. The present village was largely created by North British Railway to house its staff.*]

Pass the signal box and platform on your right and then turn right (way-marked) diagonally across a small field through a gate to a left turn along a lane opposite some **bungalows (2)** (Long distance walkers should turn left here and continue on Walk 10 towards Redesmouth Hall) and then right onto the main road (The exact Right of Way from the station is currently being contested, so the route may change). Where this turns left after about a quarter of a mile look out for a signpost "Buteland ½". Follow the direction indicated over a stile and up a steep slope, crossing a small stream "en route" to a second, waymarked stile. Continue steadily uphill aiming gradually towards the wall to your right and follow it up past a gap and a gateway to a gate ahead of

Ruin on Walk 9

you. This is marked as the end of the 'permissive path', but both the OS map and the signpost directing walkers down to Redesmouth suggest that you go through it. That done, turn right across some grass and join the road at Bute-land – and the Redesmouth signpost. Continue downhill through two gates across the road and where the latter turns left follow the direction of a 'Public Bridleway' sign over a stile past a small house and over tussocky grass into a wood. The path is indistinct here but basically continue slightly left and then right at a small derelict wooden construction, whose purpose none of our family could guess, down to Heugh Burn. Cross this and climb the opposite slope up to a stile over a fence. Keep to the right hand slopes of higher ground to your left and leave a fence a little distance to your left as well, to reach a stile over a fence ahead of you. Cross this and a narrow stream just after it and continue ahead up a slope to reach the Heugh/Buteland road junction and the end of this walk. When we explored it, the footpath sign to Buteland was lying on the ground; otherwise it would be an aiming point. If you prefer to keep drier shod you can see from the map that it is possible to do the entire walk from Redesmouth to here by road (now he tells us!).

Walk 10: Redesmouth to Bellingham (circular)

This is a most attractive and easy walk with mostly firm going, a little of it on roads, but most of it on good paths and farm roads. The outward route follows the riverbank for much of the way. Returning from Bellingham you climb to Blakelaw farm, the highest point of the walk, affording extensive views. Thereafter there is a gradual descent (with a few 'ups' after water crossings) to the delightful Rede Bridge and a final mile along the Scotsgap/Morpeth ("Wanney") railway line to Redesmouth Junction.

Distance: 7 miles (10 km) Time: 3 hours

Terrain: As per introduction, there are a few short muddy stretches, 4 stiles, 14 gates

Parking: In Redesmouth as suggested for Walk 9, in Bellingham ample parking places in the village centre

Refreshments: Bellingham – Riverdale Hotel, Cheviot Hotel, Black Bull, Rose and Crown, Fountain Cottages Tea Room at the Library/Tourist Office, and the 'Snack Bar' nearby

Start: Long distance walkers coming from the South will start/continue on their way at Redesmouth, where the walks description starts (1), however if you want to do this walk on its own, I suggest you start/finish at Bellingham with its prospect of refreshment and much more parking space. It also makes the walk available to those using the bus.

Continue a few yards North along the lane to a crossroads and turn sharp left down the road past the former Engine shed to Redesmouth Hall at the entrance to which turn right onto the road leading down to the main road at Redesmouth

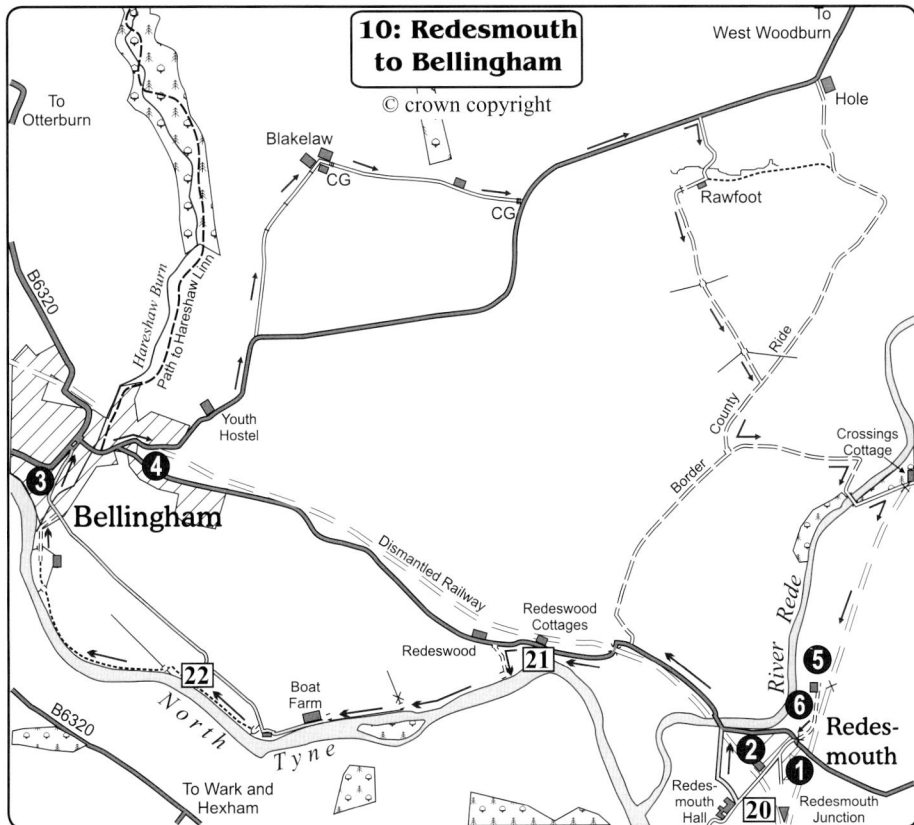

10: Redesmouth to Bellingham

© crown copyright

To Otterburn

To West Woodburn

Hole

Blakelaw
CG
CG

Rawfoot

B6320

Hareshaw Burn

Path to Hareshaw Linn

Ride

County

Border

Crossings Cottage

Youth Hostel

③ **④**

Bellingham

Dismantled Railway

Redeswood Cottages

Redeswood

⑤

⑥

River Rede

22

Boat Farm

21

North

Tyne

B6320

To Wark and Hexham

Redesmouth Hall

20

Redesmouth Junction

②

①

Redes-mouth

Bridge. As you cross notice the piers of the former railway bridge alongside the road. Keep on the road for just over half a mile, passing under a railway bridge and shortly after Redeswood Cottages, just before the larger Redeswood Farm, turn left at a "Footpath" sign, through a gate marked "Private – no unauthor-ised fishing" and follow the farm track down to the river. Turn right through a waymarked gate and follow a clear track to a stile beside a metal gate. Ahead you can either follow a permissive path through a gate to the left of a fence, or keep the right along the right of way. Either way you emerge through gates onto the metalled road at Boat Farm. Shortly after the farm turn left through a kissing gate signposted "Bellingham 1". The path continues beside the river through three more gates (the last two separated by low wooden fences as you pass through the edge of a garden). Just before Hareshaw Burn the path becomes an unmetalled road swinging right beside the Burn, follow this up to a road where a footpath sign points back to "Boat 1". Turn left and follow the road across the burn round to the right and into the centre of Bellingham, where long distance walkers might like to stop for a breather (or for the night!) before continuing on Walk 11.

[*Bellingham, for me, always has the rugged feel of a border town, which for many centuries of course it was, until the Anglo-Scottish border was finally fixed. It is a self-sufficient place with a range of shops, opportunities for refreshment, Post Office and Tourist Information. It used to have a thriving Mart before the scourge of centralisation eliminated many such local ones, but still has a very popular Agricultural Show every August.* **The Heritage Centre (4)** *is worth a visit (open Easter to October) as is the* **Church (3)**, *13th century in origin, but rebuilt in 1609. It is one of only two in England with a stone slabbed roof and the ribs of the stone ceiling vault merge into the walls, a very solid structure, perhaps with an eye to defence in time of attack? If you have time to spare, a path (see Walk Map) leads through pretty woods to Hareshaw Linn – a waterfall. The 3-mile round is ideal for a family walk. Bellingham, incidentally, is pronounced 'Bellin-jam".*]

To continue the walk (or start it if you have parked in Bellingham) turn right just past most of the shops into the West Woodburn road and continue uphill (after leaving the town) ignoring the Redesmouth road. You may wish to visit the **Heritage Centre (4)** in the former station yard. About half a mile further on where the road bears sharp right go ahead ("Pennine Way") along the farm road to Blakelaw through 3 metal gates and a double one at the farm. At the centre of the farm turn right (Pennine Way goes off to the left) and follow the farm road over two cattle grids to the West Woodburn road. Turn left. After half a mile turn right down the farm road ("Public Bridleway Rede Bridge 1½") across a stream and up to Rawfoot, where waymarks point right and left. Either route leads to the Border Country Ride. Our walk takes the right direction, through the farm to a metal gate. Turn left after it and follow the tractor track – very muddy in places – with a fence and for the last few yards a wall on your right through a metal gate and an open gateway to a boggy pasture. The Border Country Ride, another tractor trail, is straight ahead, turn right and follow it to a metal gate. Turn left onto a much firmer track, which takes you down to Rede Bridge. Incidentally don't be put off by the sound of distant explosions and small arms fire.

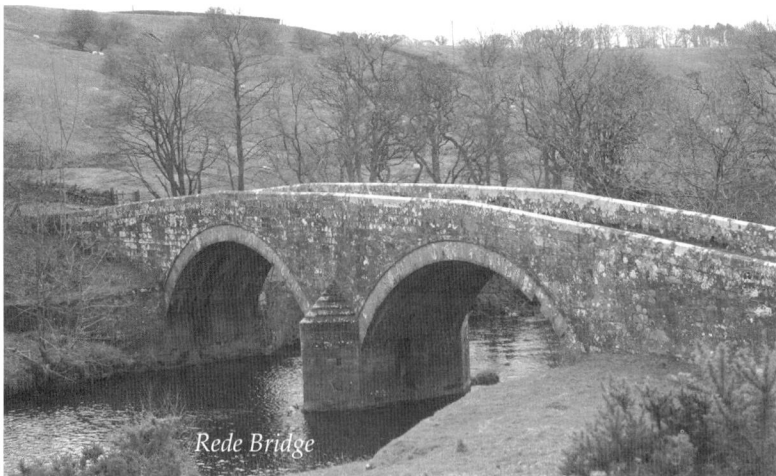

Rede Bridge

Sound travels far 'on the tops' and you are hearing Otterburn Military Ranges – they aren't gunning for you. There is a short steep climb up from Rede Bridge with a wood on your left to a four-armed signpost by Crossings Cottage, with its impressive topiary of a peacock. Turn right over a stile ("Redesmouth ½") onto the old railway track bed and continue along this to a ladder stile beside a metal gate near an **old hut (5)**. If you want a slightly longer, but probably drier walk, you could continue straight ahead at Crossings Cottage ("Redesmouth – A68 Road ½") and then turn right when you reach the road, and down to Redesmouth. Back to the railway track, this becomes very muddy just after the stile so it is advisable to climb up the low embankment on your right and as you approach a bridge move across onto the track to **Dove Cottage (6)** which brings you up, via a ladder stile, to the main road – signpost to whence you have come "Rede Bridge ¾". Turn left and then right just before the phone box to the **'bungalow' lane (1)**.

During the next walk you enter the Northumberland National Park. This is one of a family of National Parks in the UK – areas chosen for protection because of their outstanding landscapes. It is the job of the staff at the National Park Authority to conserve the special qualities of the area and to make sure that there are opportunities for people to appreciate and enjoy the Park during their visit, and, in my opinion, very well do they do it.

Walk 11: Bellingham to Charlton (circular)

Most of the outward leg is along the riverbank. After a short stretch of busy road, you climb up to 'Lonesome Pine' for wonderful views – and a good sheltered picnic spot, before returning to Bellingham along pleasant farm tracks and roads. See Walk 10 for a note about Bellingham.

Distance: 4 miles (7 km) *Time*: 2 hours
Terrain: Mostly good firm field paths, some muddy tractor tracks, some good farm roads, a short stretch of busy main road. One flight of steps, 7 stiles, 4 gates
Parking: In Bellingham village centre
Refreshments: In Bellingham – see Walk 10, information
Start: In Bellingham Square at the **Rose and Crown (1)**

On the edge of the main road opposite the **Rose and Crown (1)** a signpost points you to the "Riverside Walk. St. Cuthbert's Well". Follow the side road down to the right (facing the Rose and Crown) past Lyndale Guest House to turn right at a crossroads signposted "St. Cuthbert's Well'. Just after a garage the road becomes a path, which curves left and over an embankment to the river. Follow the path through a picnic area, under the road bridge, through a kissing gate. The fence to your right gives way to an open field shortly after a footbridge. The ground is boggy herea-

Bellingham

bouts. When the river curves away to your left a stile invites you into a scrubby wood. Although there is an exit stile at the far end, I would ignore this invitation, as the wood is overgrown and pathless. Continue instead along the low embankment skirting the fence. After the wood look across the river at the imposing frontage of Hesleyside, home of the Charltons, a prominent border family for many centuries of peace - and war. A stile takes you onto the road. Turn left. Take care as it has a good deal of fast traffic, with only narrow grass verges on which to take refuge. At the stile an optimistic sign points back to Bellingham 1. You have in fact covered 1½ miles! After ½ mile look out for a signpost on your right – "Longheughshields ¼, The Riding ¾" (at least!). [Long distance walkers continue along the road to Charlton, to join Walk 12]. Continuing this walk climb over the stile at the signpost and up a very steep hillside to a footbridge, approached by a few stone steps, over the old railway. Three sets of waymarked posts guide you uphill with a fence over to your left until you join a wall on your right with a ladder stile ahead. Cross this and, almost at once, another on your right over the wall. The right of way continues, muddily, past Longheughshields to a further ladder stile after which you turn immediately left and a steep climb takes you to 'Lonesome Pine'. This is a sheltered spot, in the corner of two walls, for a picnic while you absorb the view. [For an easier climb, there is a clearly defined track up the hill from the stile just before Longheughshields – a wooden hurdle serves as a gate through the wall at the top. This is not a right of way, but seems to be well used by walkers and joins a permissive path beyond the 'gate'.] From Lonesome Pine continue beside the wall for a few yards to a ladder stile. On the other side join a clear tractor trail which brings you down to two metal gates at The Riding. These lead you into the farm and a waymark on the second guides you to the left between buildings and out towards a **cottage (2)**, just before which look out for a stile on the left. Go over this and under a strand of wire beyond it and then head up a field. There is a line of telegraph poles ahead – aim for the one

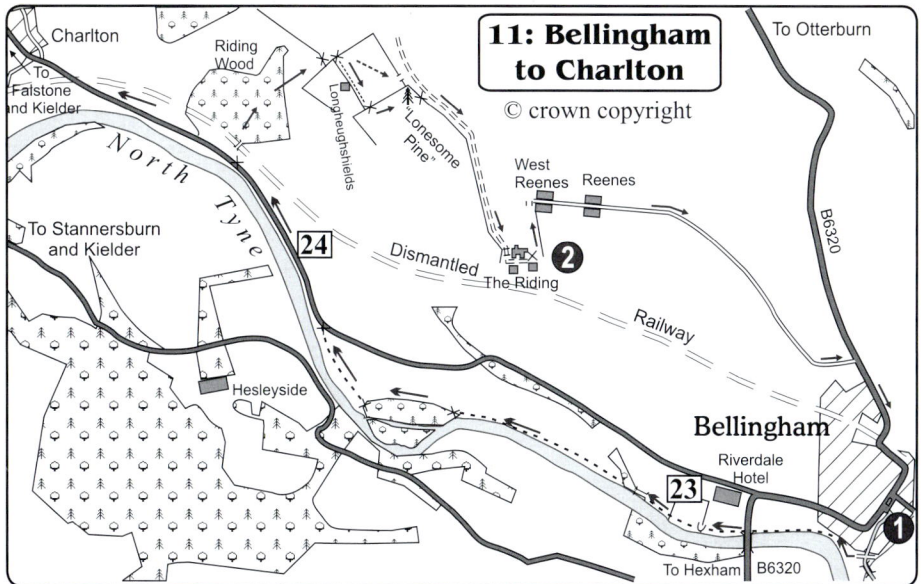

11: Bellingham to Charlton

© crown copyright

with a metal box on it. This brings you towards a wall on your right approaching in a North Westerly direction. Go through a gate at West Reenes. Turn right and follow a good farm road through Reenes, down to the B6320. Turn right to take you back into Bellingham.

Walk 12: Charlton to Lanehead (circular)

Although this attractive walk does not follow the riverbank, it affords excellent views up the North Tyne valley towards Kielder. Apart from about a mile on a moderately busy road the walk is along a quiet farm road initially, and the final section is across moorland (though mainly on farm tracks) with a chance to explore the waterfalls on Charlton Burn en-route.

Distance: 5 miles (8km) *Time*: 2½ hours
Terrain: Roads, farm roads, woodland path, some open moorland, tractor tracks, no stiles, 9 gates
Parking: In large lay-by at Charlton (1)
Refreshments: The Holly Bush at Greenhaugh (Opening times - see Walk 13) (4)
Start: At the lay-by (1)

From the lay-by head along the road in the Bellingham direction for about 100 yards then turn right onto the metalled road to Newton. You traverse two cattle grids (or the adjacent metal gates) and pass a **cottage (2)** before the road curves right at the entrance to Newton Farm. The road continues left between the buildings and the old railway line then turn right under the railway bridge

35

and immediately left along a muddy farm track. Where this comes to a gateway and wall ahead turn right and follow the wall uphill to a metal gate by a **house** (3) where you join a hard surfaced track. Follow this uphill and round to the left where just past the High Newton entrance it becomes, at a cattle grid, a fully metalled road, which takes you past Park Cottage and over another grid to the main road. [Just after the first of these grids the OS map shows a path behind Park Cottages and across the fields to Lanehead, but we stuck to the road as we could see no sign or waymarks

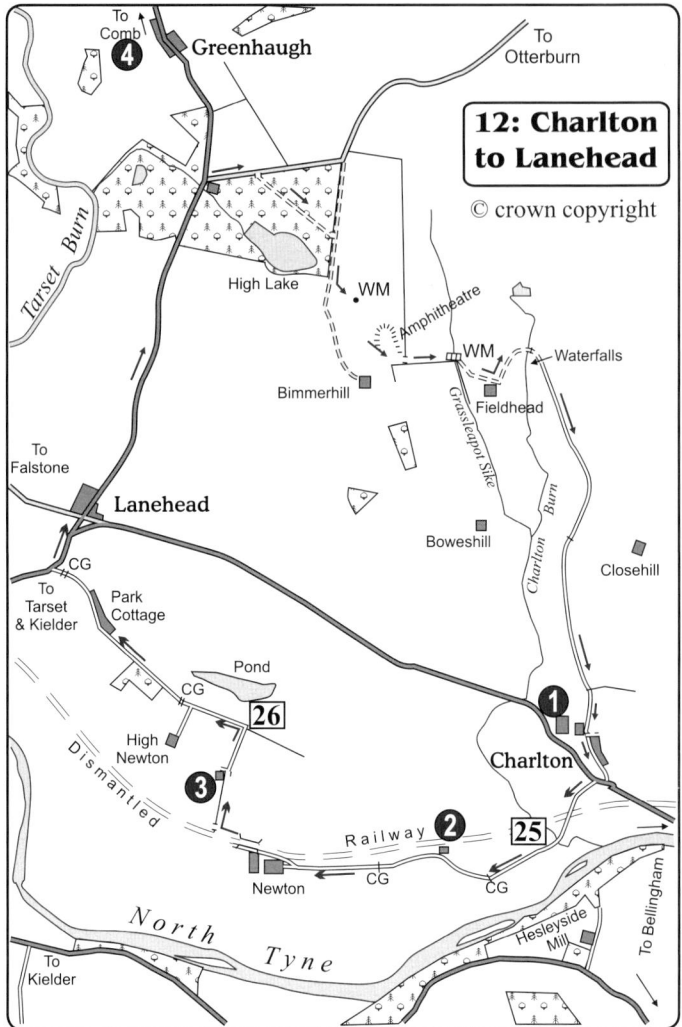

12: Charlton to Lanehead

© crown copyright

To Comb
4
Greenhaugh
To Otterburn

Tarset Burn

High Lake
WM

Amphitheatre

WM
Waterfalls

Bimmerhill
Grassleapot Sike
Fieldhead

To Falstone

Lanehead

Boweshill

Charlton Burn

Closehill

CG
To Tarset & Kielder
Park Cottage

Pond

CG
26

Dismantled
High Newton
3

Charlton

1

Railway
2
25

Newton
CG
CG

North Tyne

To Kielder

Hesleyside Mill

To Bellingham

to indicate it, but do explore it, if you prefer to be off road.] At Park Cottage you get excellent views up towards Kielder. Turn right to reach Lanehead, where you take the road signposted, more or less straight ahead to Greenhaugh and Otterburn, but long distance walkers change to Walk 13. Continue up this road for a mile to the junction where the Greenhaugh road continues ahead (the **Holly Bush Inn (4)** is ¼ mile along this road) but you turn right along the Otterburn/Elsdon road. Look out, shortly, for a footpath sign at a gate into the woods on your right. Follow this firm (except for a muddy few yards in the middle) pine-needled path to a gate, which brings you out onto a firm

36

farm track. Turn right and where the wood ends there is a waymarked post on your left. The next half mile of the walk is across quite rugged moorland, but if you follow the directions shown by the series of excellent waymarked posts ("Northumberland National Park") you should not go wrong – my wife and I didn't. Follow the left hand direction pointing to a post on the near skyline. Take in the general direction as you will lose sight of it as you go downhill slightly and then up the hillside. As the view unfolds beyond this next way-mark you will see a natural amphitheatre ahead of you, skirt the right hand edge of this to a gate in the corner of two walls and follow the wall beyond it on your right, at the end of which you descend a steep slope to cross Grasslea-pot Sike on a wooden walkway and up an equally steep slope to follow another waymark's guidance to a wide farm track. As this passes Fieldhead House a multi-arrowed waymark post gives the track uphill to your left as one option. Take it and cross Charlton Burn via a gate in a small straggly wood. Attractive waterfalls tumble down the valley to your right. Continue downhill on this clear farm track, though muddy in places, through two metal gates, the second of which guards the hamlet of Charlton. Just after the first building on your right, turn right to a waymarked metal gate, where a 'footpath' sign points back the way you have come. Turn left down a road to the main road and then right to regain your starting point.

Walk 13: Lanehead to Thorneyburn and Greenhaugh (Circular)

Although over half this walk is on road only the final mile and a half back to Lanehead has any appreciable traffic – indeed you will be lucky (or unlucky) to meet any vehicles on the rest of it. It is a lovely walk with varied scenery, some of it dramatic, as you ascend from river level up to and across Thorneyburn Common. There are a few boggy patches on the cross-country sections, but mostly firm going under normal conditions.

Distance: 7 miles (10km) Time: 3 hours
Terrain: Roads, unmade up roads, field paths, open moorland, 3 stiles, 13 gates, 4 steps
Parking: In Lanehead. If on the road, take care not to cause obstructions. There are several car-wide firm verges, but please do not harm the daffodils.
Refreshments: Greenhaugh - Holly Bush (4) (Tuesday to Sunday – evenings, Saturday & Sunday lunch)
Start: In Lanehead at the Donkleywood road end

The first mile of the walk is along the quiet Donkleywood road, crossing the substantial Tarset Burn then steadily uphill to a road junction, with a cattle grid beside it where you turn left. After a straight stretch the road bends left and then right at which point, if you want to join the riverbank for a while, follow the footpath sign to "The Hott ½ mile" left over a broken wall. Your general direction is to an arched tunnel under the old railway, but getting to it involves navigating some very marshy ground, probably by heading up the low bank to a wooden post and then scrambling down to the tunnel, which is guarded by a gate. Thereafter the path is a good one, but if you don't relish the marshy bit you can always continue along the road past the former Thorneyburn Station, whose level crossing gates are still in situ. Back at the tunnel, the path continues clearly along the top of a slope then down to the riverside fence past a hut and a footbridge, which leads across the river to the Hott. A little further on, after a kissing gate, the path turns up to an embankment (not the railway) and follows the line of a fence to emerge over a stile back onto the road just South of Thorneyburn Station.

[*One wonders how busy the station was as a glance at the OS map shows the wide scattering of 'Thorneyburn' place names, with about ten dwellings in all, and the Church and Old Rectory a mile and a half from the station. The provision of one weekday train each way (two to Hexham on Saturday) in the 1938 Bradshaw suggests not very!*]

A long straight stretch of road through sheep pasture leads to a metal gate (on the firm grassland on the left hand side of the road is the suggested parking spot for Walk 14). Beyond this gate, after the Thorney Burn bridge, look out for a signpost at a gate on your right to "Slaty Ford 1". Long distance walkers are now on Walk 14 and should continue along the road. Walk 13 continues through the gate and across the old railway at a metal gate. Climb a short steep slope ahead furrowed by many tractors. Ahead about ½ mile slightly to your right you will see Hill House, approximately at the top of a steep climb. The OS map shows the right of way zigzagging up the hill, but you should take the most direct line to the house as there is no clear path. Go through a waymarked gate, across the farm road and up some stone steps to pass through a small plantation to another gate. As you reach the fence on your right you come suddenly upon the impressive gorge of Hillhouse Clints. Shortly go right through a gate (they are all waymarked) and turn left to follow the fence, now on your left. Take care as there is a steep drop down to Thorney Burn on your right. After another gate, ahead of you, the fence curves right to a further gate, after which the path veers slightly away from the fence to the right (there is a waymarked post to guide you) before rejoining it at a short walled track leading through a gate (with a stile beside it) to the Border County Ride and Slaty Ford. Turn right to the Ford, which takes Thorney Burn across the Ride and down waterfalls into the gorge below – a good photo opportunity! Continue through a gate along the Ride, through a metal gate where a wall appears on your left. When the wall turns North turn off left across Thorneyburn Common following the direction signposted "Thorneyburn Lodge 1". Keep to the left of the first **small wood (1)** to a gate in the corner where two walls meet and

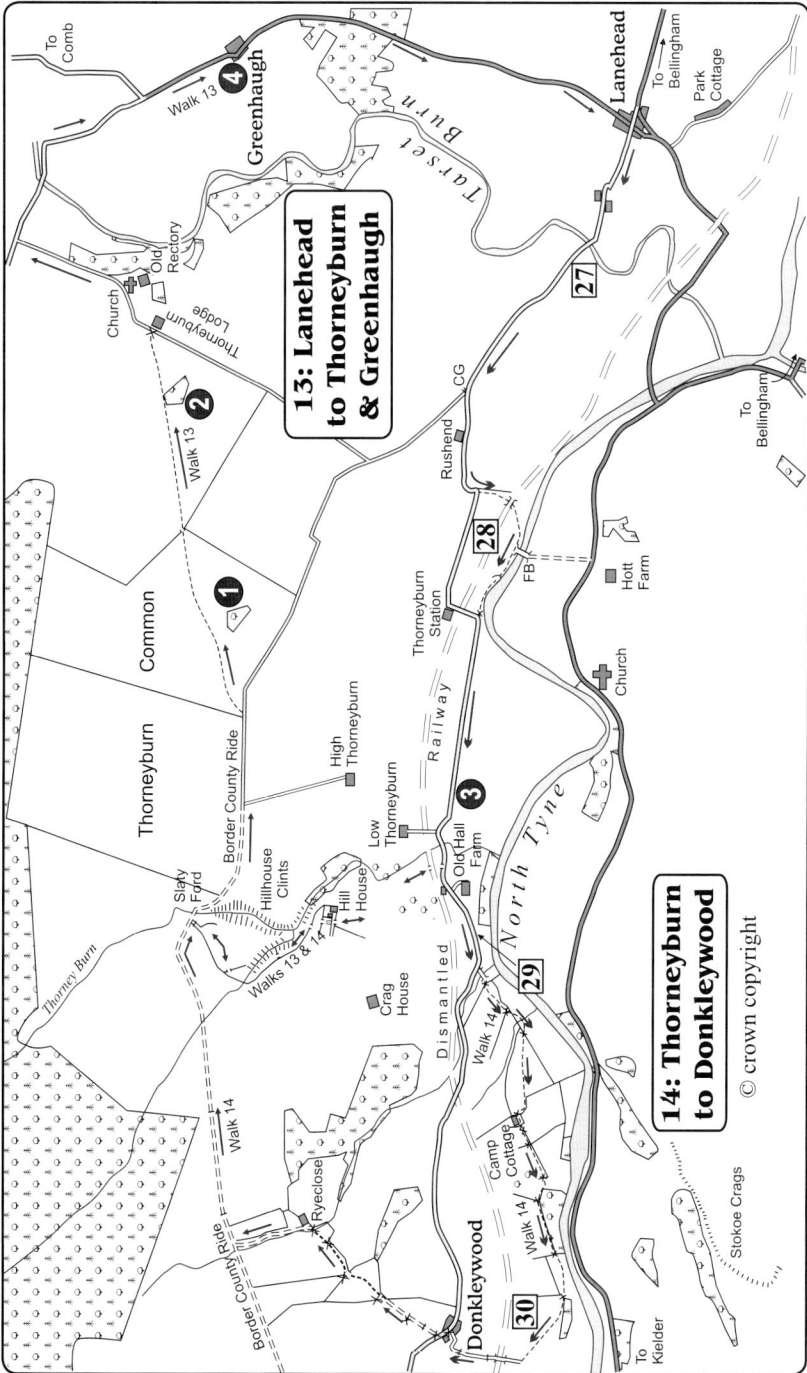

13: Lanehead to Thorneyburn & Greenhaugh

14: Thorneyburn to Donkleywood

© crown copyright

To Comb

Walk 13

Greenhaugh

Tarset Burn

Lanehead

To Bellingham

Park Cottage

Old Rectory

Church

Thorneyburn Lodge

Walk 13

CG

Rushend

To Bellingham

Thorneyburn Common

High Thorneyburn

Thorneyburn Station

Hott Farm

Church

Railway

Border County Ride

Low Thorneyburn

North Tyne

Slaty Ford

Hillhouse Clints

Hill House

Walks 13 & 14

Old Hall Farm

Crag House

Dismantled

Thorney Burn

Walk 14

Walk 14

Ryeclose

Border County Ride

Camp Cottage

Walk 14

Donkleywood

Stokoe Crags

To Kielder

FB

27

28

29

30

1

2

3

4

on to pass along the edge of the next **small wood (2)** to a stile opposite the left hand end of Thorneyburn Lodge signposted back to "High Thorneyburn 1¼". There is a farm track leading up to the midpoint gate, but in the main you have to follow the general direction indicated across the Common as I could find no certain path. Turn left onto the road past the Lodge and continue past the Church to a road junction, turn right and follow this road through Greenhaugh to join the main road coming in on your left from Otterburn and downhill back to Lanehead.

[At Thorneyburn Church you will see a path signposted to Greenhaugh. When I later explored it this proved quite a challenging path, not consistently way marked, and with a good deal of scrambling up and down uneven slopes. I haven't included it, but, if you have your OS map, you might like to test your map reading! As this a long walk, I felt it preferable to finish along the road – passing the Holly Bush!]

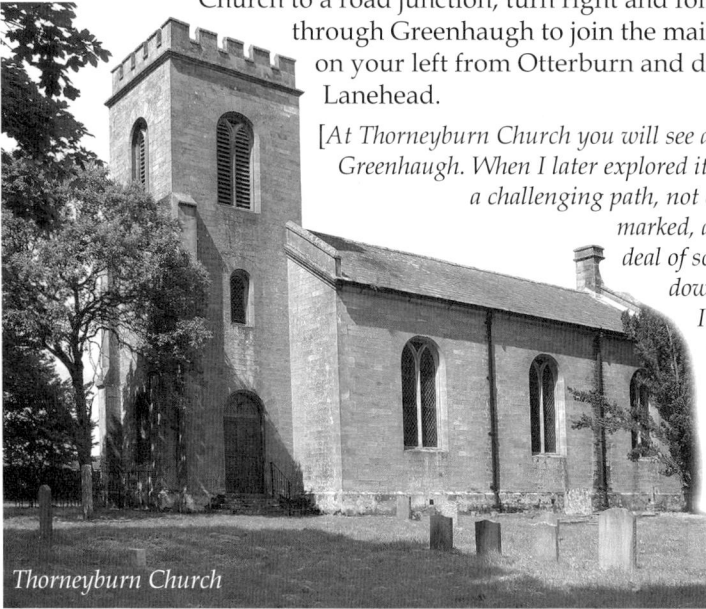

Thorneyburn Church

Walk 14: Thorneyburn to Donkleywood (Circular)

What might be termed a 'stilish' walk (16 stiles in all!), no. 14 is almost entirely off road. It follows the river initially then stikes uphill through Donkleywood to the Border County Ride. At Slaty Ford it shares Walk 13's route downhill back to the start. Some muddy patches, but firm going on the whole.

Distance: 4½ miles (7 km) Time: 2 hrs
Terrain: Short distance of road, field paths, hard surface Border County Ride, 18 gates, 16 stiles
Parking: At Thorneyburn, on a grass-land beside road near metal gate (3)
Refreshments: None (nearest see Walk 13 or 15)
Start: Where you have parked

Go through the metal gate, along the road and about ¼ mile beyond Oldhall Farm turn off the road at a signpost "Donkleywood 1½" and follow a path (in places more of a rivulet) down to a footbridge and up to the first of a series of stiles (all waymarked). Cross a field (fence on your left) to the next and then, with a fence now on your right, over a small stream to a third stile to your right. A clear path leads across a field to a metal gate to the right of which a stile beckons you round the South side of Camp Cottage to a gate and adjacent stile. Turn left and shortly over two stiles separated by a line of tress. Another stile brings you to the edge of a wood with a steep slope down to the river. Three more stiles punctuate a clear path above the river and finally across a boggy field to the farm road leading over the railway bridge up to Donkley-wood, passing through two metal gates 'en route'. While it seems obvious to follow the short stretch of farm road to the 'main' road, there is a ladder stile to the left between two buildings, which is the right of way. Just beyond it a sign-post points back to "Camp Cottage 1". Turn left, and if you are a long distance walker continue along the road to Falstone and Hawkhope (Link Walk 15). To continue this walk almost at once follow the direction "Ryeclose ½" on your right over a stile beside a double metal gate. Then up a wide gravelled track through two more metal gates, the second of which has an adjacent stile. Just before a fourth metal gate turn left through a muddy patch of field to a wide stile over a fence (my O.S. map is not quite up to date re recent fencing herea-bouts, but the path is well waymarked.) Go North East across the next field to another stile beside a gateway. Aim then for Ryeclose, a stretch of tractor track provides some guidance. A stile and a ladder stile take you onto the Ryeclose farm road. Turn left and through a gate along the road to a large wooden gate leading onto the Border County Ride. Turn right and follow this, through two gates, to Slaty Ford. Ignore the signpost to Sidwood off to your left, but shortly turn right into a wettish short, walled track signposted "Hillhouse ½". You are now following part of Walk 13. After a stile beside a gate, a fence bears off to your right, seemingly in the wrong direction, so it is tempting to follow the wall on your left. Don't, as this will take you to the edge of deep Hillhouse Clint, so turn right and follow the path slightly to the left of the fence. There is a way marked post to guide you. Just where you rejoin the fence you reach a gate. The fence now gradually curves round left along the edge of the impres-sive chasm of Hillhouse Clint. The path skirts the fence through another gate – take care as there is a steep drop to your left. The next gate takes you over the fence which you now follow, briefly, to another gate leading to a small plantation. You then go down stone steps across the Hillhouse farm road and through a gate into a wide stretch of pasture going downhill. Keep to the left of a lone tree and aim for a slightly uphill slope furrowed by tractor tracks between two clumps of trees. This will bring you to a metal gate at the old railway line. Cross it and shortly afterwards a gate (signed, whence you have come, "Slaty Ford 1") leads onto the road. Turn left and return to where you have parked.

Walk 15 (Link): Donkleywood to Falstone (Linear)

This is a pleasant undemanding road and forest road link between Walks 14 and 16 for long distance walkers. It finishes at Hawkhope Car Park (5) and would, for example, provide a 10 mile walk from Bellingham. I have not put in a Parking suggestion, as you will probably have begun at the start of an earlier walk.

Falstone

Continue from Donkleywood along the road past **Falstone Station (4)** to the village and where the road turns left continue straight ahead along the forest road ("Forestry vehicles only") to Hawkhope Car Park, the approach to which by car is the road along the top of the dam.

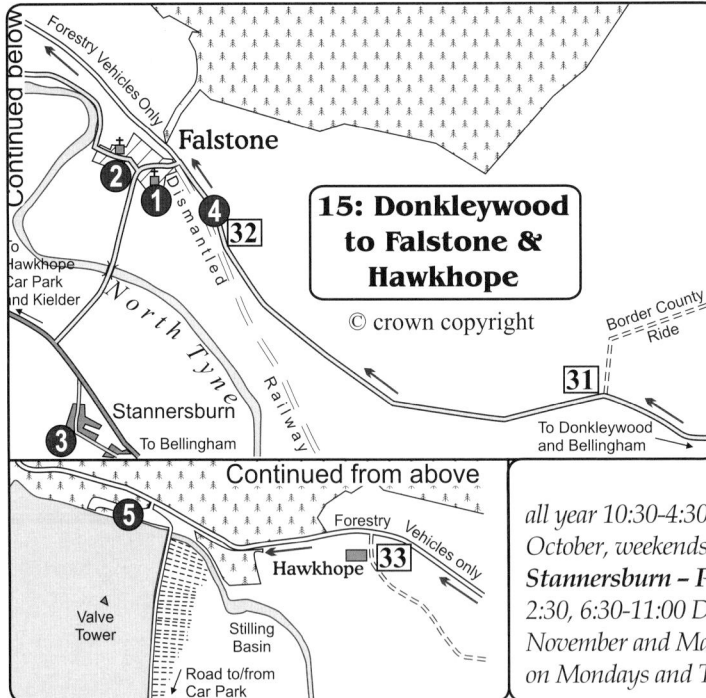

15: Donkleywood to Falstone & Hawkhope

© crown copyright

Distance (one way): 3 miles (5 km) Time: 1 hr

Terrain: No gates or stiles

Refreshments: Falstone – Blackcock Inn (1) Mon 7-11pm Tues - closed, Wed-Fri 7-11, Sat/Sun 12-3, 7-11/10:30, Old School Tea Room (2) Open all year 10:30-4:30 Daily Easter to October, weekends only in Winter, Stannersburn – Pheasant (3) 12:00-2:30, 6:30-11:00 Daily except between November and March when it closes on Mondays and Tuesdays.

42

Kielder Water and Forest Park: *Kielder Water was created between 1976 and 1982 to provide a constant water supply to industrial Teeside. A pumping station at Riding Mill (5 miles downstream from Hexham) fed an underground aqueduct to Teeside, which is still regularly checked by sub-terranean cycling inspectors. As Kielder's industrial purpose has contracted, so its leisure facilities expanded. Its ever increasing recreational experiences include self-guided walking and cycling trails, fishing, artworks, water sport, ferry cruises, sailing, wildlife and local heritage.*

There are three visitors' centres at Tower Knowe, Leaplish and Kielder Castle, with a wide range of activities (see Walk 16 for locations).

Last, but by now means least, Kielder Water's 41,350 million gallons of water ensures that drought is unlikely to be a problem in the Tyne Valley – yet another reason to visit us!

Kielder Forest: *This is one of the largest forests in Europe specifically planted by man. Since its inception after the First World War to produce a strategic timber reserve the focus has changed to one of multi-purpose management, though with timber remaining the primary source of income. This has allayed much of the early criticism by sheep farmers and lovers of our wild moorland who did not want to lose their open spaces - and of course you only have to climb Peel Fell or sample Walks 8 or 9 in this book to see that we still have miles of open moorland to explore. In fact the Forestry Commission's, sensitive management, including a leavening of conifers with broadleaved trees has improved the habitat of the wide range of local wildlife and enhanced much of the landscape, producing in places, more agricultural land than before. The leisure facilities for the half million annual visitors to the Forest Park are described above, but so large is the area that many times that number could be welcomed to Kielder without it becoming over-crowded. But it does remain a working forest. Once the first trees were planted in 1926 and felling and replanting began in 1948, this has been a continuous cycle of work. 50 lorry loads of timber are produced each day and about 3 million trees replanted each year. If you would like to see the Forest at work phone the Forestry Commission on 01434 220242 to arrange a visit.*

Kielder Water from Elf Kirk

Walk 16: Falstone/ Hawkhope to Kielder

Although it is possible to reach this walk in the summer and on certain days of the week, by public transport, that needs some ingenuity, so it is best done by using two cars – one at each end. The first half of the walk could be extended to a circular walk via Plashetts Incline and Benny Shank (see text), but at the time of writing the 2 miles from Benny Shank back round Whinny Hill is blocked by gale felled trees and not recommended until they are cleared, which is a priority for the Forestry Commission but will take time, as the path is not readily accessible to wheeled vehicles, though very well waymarked for walkers throughout. I hope all the above hasn't put you off the linear walk, which though largely on the North Haul Road, a hard surface forest road, well used by Forestry vehicles, is an increasingly attractive walk with extensive views of Kielder Water and suitable for pushchairs throughout.

Distance: 7½ miles (12 km) Time: 2½ hrs *(The Hawkhope/Plashetts Incline/Benny Shank round, when restored, would be 9 miles (15 km) and take about 4 hours.*

Terrain: *See above. There is also a short flight of steps at Kielder.*

Parking: *Hawkhope and Kielder (both Pay and Display). Do not use the Forestry road from Falstone to Hawkhope. The approach to Hawkhope Car Park is along the top of the dam and which joins the Bellingham-Kielder road between Stannersburn and Tower Knowe.*

Refreshments: *At Falstone, see Walk 15:* **Kielder Castle Duke's Pantry** *(9-5 or 6 weekends),* **Anglers Arms** *(12-3 pm, 6-11 pm daily). If you are travelling between Kielder and Hawkhope on the main road there are also well signed turn offs to* **Leaplish Waterside Park, Boat Inn**: *April to June, September-October 11-6, later some evenings (01434 240400) July/August 11am-11pm,* **Tower Knowe Water Edge Restaurant and Tea Room**.

Start: *Hawkhope Car Park*

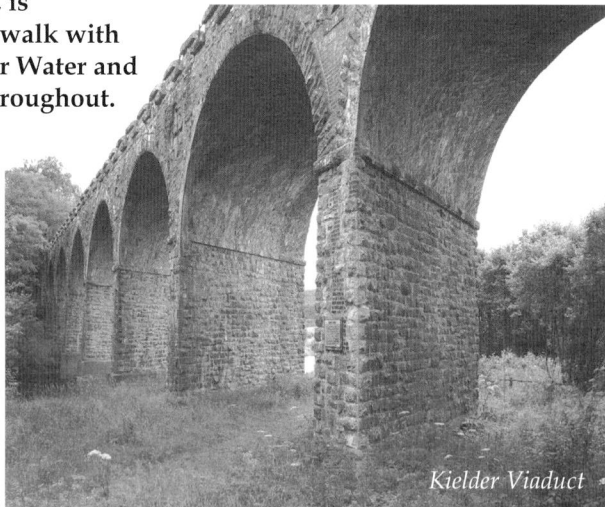

Kielder Viaduct

At the western end of the Car Park take the waymarked path (all the waymarks on this walk are broad orange arrows) to your right, the short distance up to North Haul Road. Turn left. You can continue along the road all the way to Kielder (follow Cycle Routes **6** and **10** signs ini-

44

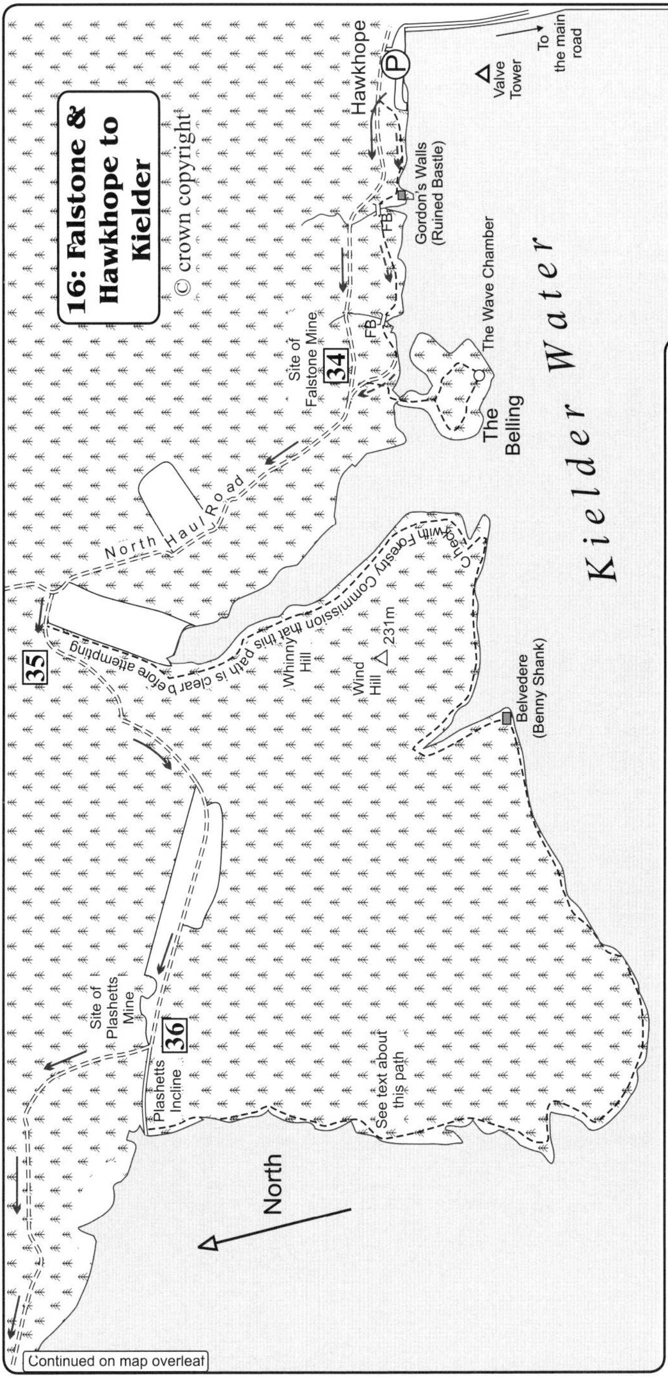

16: Falstone & Hawkhope to Kielder
© crown copyright
Hawkhope
P
To the main road
Valve Tower
To Hawk-hope and Bellingham
Tower Knowe
To Kielder
Gordon's Walls (Ruined Bastle)
FB
FB
The Wave Chamber
Kielder Water
Site of Falstone Mine
34
The Belling
North Haul Road
Check with Forestry Commission that this path is clear before attempting
Whinny Hill
Wind Hill
231m
Belvedere (Benny Shank)
35
36
Site of Plashetts Mine
Plashetts Incline
See text about this path
North
Continued on map overleaf

tially, and later just **6**). However a more interesting diversion for the first ¾ mile is to follow the way-marked path you will shortly see, leading to the water's edge. When this meets a wider track leading back up to the North Haul Road, you can either take the latter or do the short walk round the Belling, signposted "Wave Chamber". If you had stayed on the road, you would have passed the entrance to the former Falstone Mine. Continue along the road which now turns North to circumvent a long inlet of the reservoir. Where Cycle Route **(10)** continues ahead turn left **(Route 6)** round the head of the inlet. Just over a

mile after a long straight stretch of road you will see Plashetts Incline. Continue ahead where our walk veers round to the right. [*The metalled incline was the track bed of the colliery line taking coal down to the old railway at the now submerged Plashetts Station*]. You might like to take the short walk down to the water's edge where you can pick up the summer ferry service. The waymarked path to the Belvedere at Benny Shank (a sheltered viewpoint across the lake) branches off left – a very pleasant walk, but see this walk's introduction. Continuing along the road on Walk 16, about a mile beyond Plashetts at Blackarm Knowe our road curves left (look out for the Route **(6)** sign). About two miles further on and half a mile past Gowanburn, where the road becomes metalled, look out for a waymark off to the left, which leads you down steps onto the trackbed of the old railway, which emerges eerily and nostalgically from the lake. Continue along the trackbed and over **Kielder Viaduct (3)** [*Built in 1862 this is the finest surviving example of a skewed arched bridge. Each stone is individually crafted*]. Immediately beyond the bridge take the steep path down to your right and then turn left along the broad firm path across a road and on beside the river to join the main road at Kielder Castle. Turn left then immediately right over the river bridge with the **Anglers Arms (2)** on your left. **Kielder Castle (1)** is well worth a visit with a range of attractions for all ages. It is open daily, Easter to October 10am – 5pm, November weekends 11am – 4pm and December daily up to Christmas 11am – 4pm. (Kielder Castle was built in 1772 as a shooting lodge for the Duke of Northumberland). The walk ends at the car park a little further up the hill from the castle.

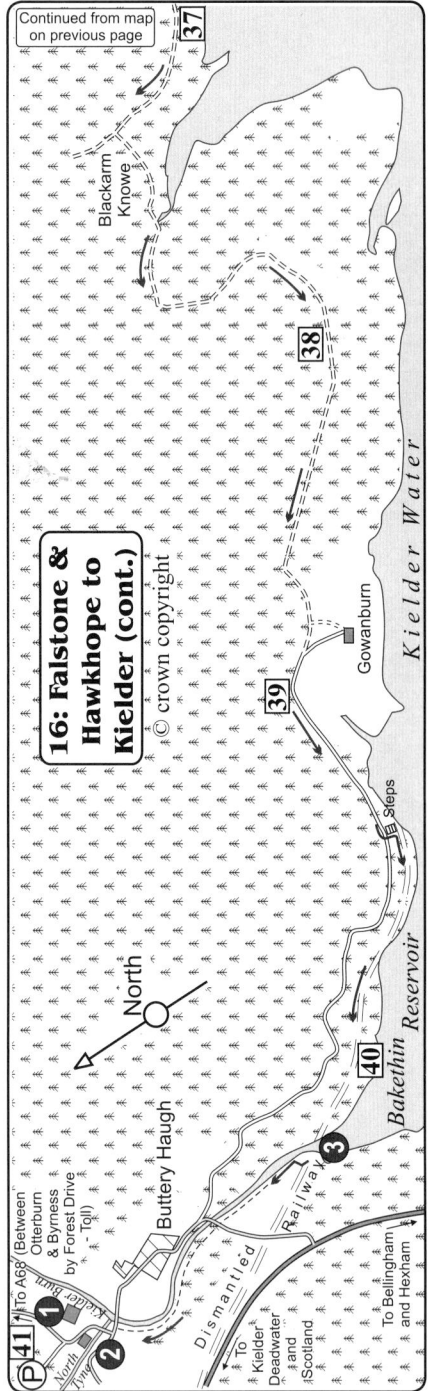

46

Continued from map on previous page

37

Blackarm Knowe

38

16: Falstone & Hawkhope to Kielder (cont.)

© crown copyright

Kielder Water

Gowanburn

39

Steps

North

Bakethin Reservoir

Buttery Haugh

40

3

Railway

Dismantled

To A68 (Between Otterburn & Byrness by Forest Drive - Toll)

Kielder Burn

North Tyne

To Kielder Deadwater and Scotland

To Bellingham and Hexham

P 41

1

2

Walk 17: Kielder to Deadwater and Source of the North Tyne

This easy and attractive walk takes you as near as you can get to the source of the North Tyne – see note below. From near Deadwater you can join the Kielder Stone Walk (see walk's description) up to the summit of Peel Fell whence you get

Distance: 7 miles (10 km) Time: 2½ hours
Terrain: Road, forest road, railway trackbed, all good hard surfaces though the trackbed can be wet and muddy in a few places. No stiles. 3 gates.
Parking: At Kielder – see Walk 16.
Start: At the car park

splendid views on a clear day including the Solway Firth and, reputedly, the North Sea – a rare chance to see both coasts from the same spot. The latest version of OS Sheet Outdoor Leisure 42 unfortunately no longer shows the route, though it is quite well waymarked. A note of warning though. It is a strenuous 12 mile round back to Kielder, with steep climbs and two miles of really boggy going (a path is non-existent) between Peel and Deadwater Fells, and certainly not to be attempted unless properly equipped, experienced and not alone as there is mobile phone reception at the very top of the Fell, but currently nowhere else 'en route'. Consult the weather forecasts, too, before setting off.

Last lap! At the far (North Western) end of the top section of the Car Park follow the Kielder Stone Path up and left towards a wooden fence linking two sections of wall, with a field beyond. Turn right and follow the wall up to a wide forest road onto which turn left. Follow it uphill at first and then down, passing where the Stone Path leaves it on the right. Continue over a cattle grid below Lightpipe and round left down to a cattle grid, a bridge over the river and the main road. Turn right and about half a mile further on where the road turns right to cross the river, turn left onto the railway track bed and immediately right (A "Cycle Route 7" waymark points you along the track) to Bellsburn cottage. Follow the track bed through a gate, another one at Bellsburnfoot and a third a mile further on where you cross Deadwater Burn. The next gate is at Deadwater Station. Turn right just before it, down the lane to the main road – and now for the source. There are several opinions, I gather, about where it actually is, and I am indebted to Mr. Jimmy Hall, who farms Deadwater Farm, and has lived there all his life, for taking me onto his land and showing me the exact spot – and most people to whom I have spoken agree with his location. There are other streams which feed the Tyne in this area, notably Kielder Burn and Deadwater Burn, which are longer and of greater volume than the stream that emerges at Deadwater, but they are tributaries. You will see on the O.S.Map that the stream appears to continue a little further North from the spot I have marked, but Mr. Hall tells me that these last few yards often dry up in summer so the spot I have marked on the walk map is the all-the-year round source of the North Tyne. As it is on private farm land the nearest you can get is to turn left and walk a few yards to the field gate or perhaps to where the woodland borders the road – a Border in two senses as Scotland begins here. You will see the tiny stream emerging from the field and where the wood curves round to the left a hundred yards or so away is the source, a spring in the side of a defile in the field. So now you must retrace your steps and continue down the road to Kielder (or beyond) and it still impresses me that only a dozen miles downstream that rivulet has already become a substantial river – I don't think that, under normal conditions, its passage through Kielder Water has altered the volume of water that emerges at Falstone.

To return to our walk, continue along the road (I understand the Forestry Commission may develop an alternative path parallel to the road in the woodland to your left, but the road isn't busy and provides a pleasant walk) until you have returned to Bellsburn, turn off the road and onto the railway line, but this time of course turn left. After exactly a mile, a track crosses the railway line from Catcleugh to the main road, over which it continues as a cul-de-sac serving three houses. Turn left along the track, but only as far as the main road. Turn right and follow it the short distance to Castle Drive off to your left through Kielder Village. Take this road, which joins the main Kielder approach road, which shortly takes you left over the river, past the **Anglers Arms (2)** and **Kielder Castle (1)** (at either or both of which you might like to stop!), and on to your starting point.

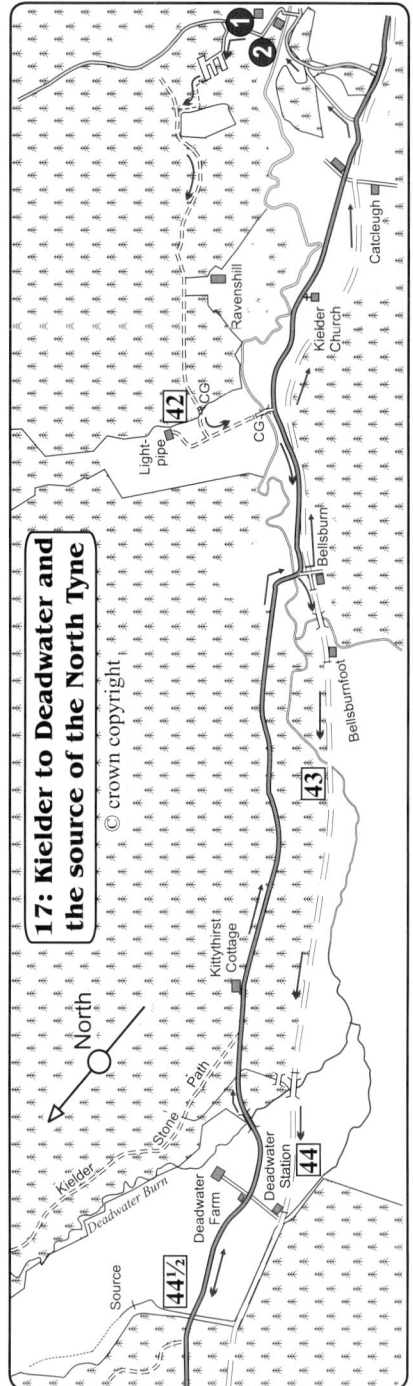

17: Kielder to Deadwater and the source of the North Tyne

© crown copyright

North

Light-pipe

CGf

42

Ravenshill

Kielder Church

Catcleugh

Bellsburn

CGf

Bellsburnfoot

Bellsburnfoot

43

Kittyhirst Cottage

Stone Path

Source

Kielder

Deadwater Burn

Deadwater Burn

Deadwater Farm

Deadwater Station

44

44½